INDOOR CAT

How to Enrich Their Lives and Expand Their World

LAURA J. MOSS
and LYNN BAHR, DVM

RUNNING PRESS
PHILADELPHIA

Running Press
Hachette Book Group
1290 Avenue of the Americas, New York, NY 10104
www.runningpress.com
@Running_Press

Printed in China

First Edition: April 2022

Published by Running Press, an imprint of Perseus Books, LLC, a
subsidiary of Hachette Book Group, Inc. The Running Press name and
logo is a trademark of the Hachette Book Group.

The Hachette Speakers Bureau provides a wide range of authors for
speaking events. To find out more, go to
www.hachettespeakersbureau.com or call (866) 376-6591.

The publisher is not responsible for websites (or their content) that are
not owned by the publisher.

Print book cover and interior design by Rachel Peckman
Cover photograph copyright © 2021 Getty Images

Library of Congress Control Number: 2021936567

ISBNs: 978-0-7624-7465-3 (hardcover), 978-0-7624-7463-9 (ebook)

RRD-S

10 9 8 7 6 5 4 3 2 1

This one's for Foxxie and Rudolph,
the first felines to steal our hearts.
And it's for everyone who picks up this book
so they can give their cat the best nine lives.

CONTENTS

INTRODUCTION

Are We Giving Our Cats the Nine Lives They Deserve?

Imagine that you could live in the home of your dreams. Within those walls, you have everything you could possibly need: Your plate is never empty, you can nap to your heart's content, you receive ample love and affection—and also plenty of delicious treats. The only catch? You can never venture beyond those walls to walk on grass, breathe fresh air, bask in direct sunlight, or interact with the world outside the window. For the rest of your life, your entire universe is confined to the space within those walls.

For the average domestic cat in America, this lifestyle isn't just a scenario; it's reality. And while a life free from the stresses of daily survival may sound idyllic, the truth is that the indoor environments we provide our feline friends often actually create entirely new stressors that threaten their mental and physical well-being. It's a sad truth that veterinarian Dr. Lynn Bahr has witnessed firsthand in her 28-year career as she watched cats move indoors and be forced to adapt to life inside four walls.

She started noticing more and more cats exhibiting signs of boredom and depression, and hearing cat owners complain about behavioral problems. These cats often had accompanying physical ailments, like obesity, diabetes, and cystitis (inflammation of the bladder), and had to be put on special diets or prescription medications. The cats that had trouble adjusting to indoor life were often prescribed human behavioral medications, declawed, rehomed, abandoned, or relinquished to shelters, and Lynn realized that millions of perfectly healthy cats were actually being euthanized because of their inability to overcome their instincts and adapt to an unnatural life.

Recognizing that indoor cats' needs weren't being met—and that cat owners often don't even understand their pets' needs—Lynn launched Dezi & Roo, a company named after her own two beloved felines. Dezi & Roo designs, manufactures, and sells solution-based pet products. Her creations aim to enhance the lives of cats and strengthen their bond with their human companions because, after all, cat owners do want what's best for their furry friends.

In fact, that's the reason many people choose to keep their cats indoors. They want their cats to be safe, and they want them to live long, happy lives. And cats certainly can live full, enriched lives indoors; however, this requires a commitment on behalf of the cat's caregiver that goes beyond simply filling the food bowl and emptying the litter box.

Unfortunately, though, the belief that cats are easy, low-maintenance pets permeates American culture. Popular wisdom holds that cats don't require outdoor time, that they can be left alone for days at a time, as long as enough food and water is left out, and that they don't need much interaction, companionship, or socialization, if any at all. In other words, "Don't have time to care for a dog? Get a cat!"

However, this widely held misbelief about cats has enabled us to treat them more as ornaments in our homes than as animals, when they're actually more closely linked to wild animals than even canines. While dogs have been domesticated over thousands of years, so-called domestic cats aren't actually that far removed genetically from their wildcat relatives. According to a study by Washington University's Genome Institute, the cats we share our homes with retain many of the hunting, sensory, and digestive traits of their wild kin. As few as 13 genes may separate domestic cats from their ancestors, and biologists have noted that cats don't meet all the criteria for domestication and may best be described as "exploited captives," according to a 2016 *Scientific World Journal* article.

So, we've taken an animal with an instinctual need to engage its highly evolved senses and confined it to a predictable, artificial environment with little to no enrichment whatsoever. In turn, our cats tend to respond in one of two ways: They act out, or they don't act at all—instead sleeping much of the day away.

Interestingly, for cats that act out—whether it's through aggression or elimination outside the litter box, among other unwanted behaviors—veterinarians and feline behaviorists often recommend environmental enrichment. In other words, simply give your cat something to do, such as introducing daily training sessions, implementing food-foraging techniques, and learning how to engage all types of cats in appropriate play. Many also suggest providing cats with outdoor opportunities, such as stroller rides, leashed walks, or access to outdoor enclosures known as "catios."

For example, when Laura noticed a trend of more and more indoor cats venturing outside in a variety of ways, she discovered that some cat owners felt it was unfair or even cruel to deprive their beloved pets of access to fresh air and sunshine, while others were strapping their cats into harnesses as a result of a veterinary recommendation or a realization that their pets required something that an indoor lifestyle simply couldn't provide.

As Laura learned more about how indoor cats can blossom and actually overcome mental and physical ailments when allowed outdoor time, it inspired her to launch AdventureCats.org, the first resource that provides information on how to enjoy the great outdoors with your cat. As Adventure Cats' social media followers grew to hundreds of thousands, Laura discovered that countless people were already adventuring with their cats or were curious about how they could

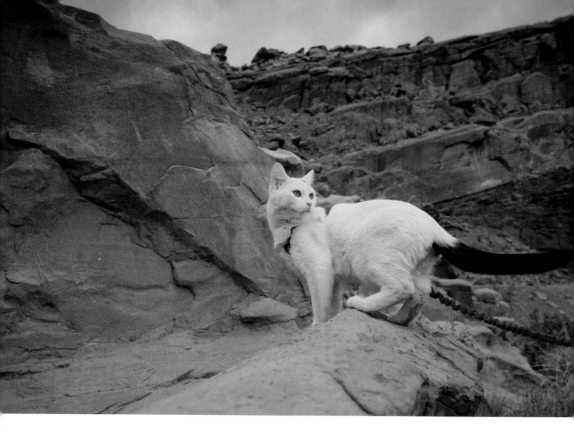

share the sights, scents, and sounds of nature with their feline friends to give them a full life.

She interviewed numerous conscientious cat owners who saw how their cats were fascinated by the world outside the window or simply struggling to adapt to living in a small space or deal with their excess energy. These cat owners told her that giving their cat the opportunity to go outside and truly be a cat—to explore, stalk, prowl, and experience the world—transformed their animals. The cats were stimulated and more active, and, in turn, they were happier and healthier.

While venturing outdoors certainly isn't a cure-all for what ails every feline, it's been widely researched and accepted by veterinary and feline behavioral experts that indoor life can be detrimental to cats' mental and physical health. By trapping our cats indoors, taking away their choices, and depriving them of opportunities to tap into their natural instincts, we're preventing them from truly being cats.

Luckily, cat owners can be responsible and compassionate caregivers while still allowing their cherished pets to be the wild animals they are at heart. However, to do this, we must first learn how to see and experience the world as our cats do because while we may think we've created the ideal feline home, the reality may be very different from a cat's perspective. That's why each chapter of this book begins by detailing the drastically antithetical viewpoints a cat owner and a cat may have about the same issue. Because once we understand the cat's point of view, we can then start making changes in our cats' environments, as well as in our interactions with our feline friends to improve their happiness and well-being.

We must also dispel the myths that harm our indoor cats, such as the widely held belief that they live twice as long as outdoor cats; the idea that declawed cats can live normal, healthy lives; and the notion that all cats crave physical affection from their caregivers, among many others. Throughout these pages you'll be introduced to scientific evidence and firsthand accounts from cat owners that will challenge your long-held beliefs about felines and will inspire you to take strides to make your own cat's life more fulfilling and enjoyable.

Each chapter of this book will delve into a particular aspect of indoor cats' lives and reveal not only how their current lifestyle may harm them, but also offer specific actions you can take to improve your cat's life. Not only can cats be trained, but you'll also learn how to incorporate training into your daily routine. You'll discover that there's a "purrfectly" valid reason your cat doesn't like to be held and how you can work with him or her to overcome those barriers to affection. You'll also realize that many, if not all, the behavioral issues you've experienced with your cat can be easily fixed and even completely avoided by making a few small changes. And you'll get "expurrt" advice that you won't find anywhere else from veterinarians, behaviorists, and other feline authorities. (All quotes were taken from interviews unless otherwise specified.)

And, finally, to truly provide our cats with the best nine lives possible we must take away the shame associated with allowing them to venture beyond the confines of our homes. The idea of permitting our treasured companion animals to step outside can be understandably nerve-racking, but we'll outline the training techniques and safety precautions necessary to ensure that your cat remains healthy, happy, and safe both indoors and out. Because by simply opening the door—or even a window—we can open up our cats' world and truly give them the life they deserve.

CHAPTER 1

The Feline "Purrspective"

Your POV: My cat is safe and happy and has everything he needs.	**Kitty POV:** But I need more than this to truly be happy.

The fact that you're holding this book means that you're already well versed in the ways of the cat. You know what it's like to maintain your balance while a furball weaves between your legs. You know the tickle of whiskers, the warm pressure of kneading paws, and the rumble of a purr in your ear. You've been awakened by the zoomies in the wee hours of the morning, and you've fallen back asleep contorting your limbs around the snoozing form of your furry friend. You certainly know all about toe beans and sun puddles and tiny triangle noses. And, let's be honest, you probably never go to the bathroom alone.

There's no doubt you've tried to give your kitty the best life possible—one might say it's even an enviable life. After all, it's not uncommon to hear cat owners declare that they'd love to live the pampered life of their beloved cat. Endless days of laziness and snoozing, interrupted only occasionally for a meal or a head scratch? It certainly sounds like a life worthy of envy.

However, while we may view the average indoor housecat's life as one where they don't *have* to do anything, the reality is that, for most cats, there's simply nothing to do. For most indoor cats, life is an endless series of days that all look exactly the same. As humans, we understand that when there's no purpose, activity, or stimuli in your daily life; when there's nothing to look forward to, no reason to wake up, it's easy to feel down, become stagnant, or even experience depression. The same goes for our feline friends.

So as much as you think you might enjoy switching places with your cat, it's likely that the novelty would wear off pretty quickly. Those catnaps you envied would soon become less about catching up on much-needed rest and more about simply passing time. Those daily treats would become less about satisfying hunger and more about merely requiring something to break up the monotony of your day.

Sounds rather depressing, right? But in order to make our cats happy and truly give them the best life, we first must see what life is like from their "purrspective" and gain an understanding of what life as an indoor cat is really about.

Meet *Felis Interius*

In many Westernized countries, it's typical for cats to live both indoors and out. For example, in the United Kingdom, only about 10 percent of pet cats are believed to live indoors permanently, according to International Cat Care, a UK-based nonprofit that works to improve felines' welfare across the globe. However, in the United States, the vast majority of pet cats are kept indoors, and the American Veterinary Medical Association encourages cat owners to keep their pets inside.

While some felines adapt to an indoor-only lifestyle easily, others may struggle to do so, and the felines that don't are often relinquished or returned to shelters, where they face a high likelihood of euthanasia. In other words, we may be unwittingly creating an entirely new breed of cat through natural selection: *felis interius*, a term we've coined for a species that's more of an ornament in our homes than it is a cat.

We can think of this breed as drastically different from a natural cat in numerous ways and identify *felix interius* by the following characteristics, which we'll explore in greater detail below:

- Often separated from its mother and littermates with limited maternal upbringing
- Housed in four walls in an unenriching environment
- Has limited ability to explore and tap into natural curiosity
- Never breathes fresh air—only climate-controlled air
- Has no access to direct sunlight
- Has never walked on grass or soil—walks exclusively on carpet or flooring
- Is inactive and lacks sufficient exercise
- Sleeps 16–20 hours a day
- Is fed an artificial diet in the same location
- Uses a box to urinate and defecate
- Is often declawed
- May suffer from certain mental and physical health issues
- May have several different owners as it's rehomed, relinquished, or abandoned

I Didn't Get It from My Mama

In shelter and rescue environments, kittens are often removed from their mother's care once they've been weaned, which is typically at only six weeks to eight weeks of age. However, although kittens can eat on their own at this time, that doesn't necessarily mean they're ready to leave their mother's care, because there's still much to learn.

"Kittens orphaned or separated from their mother and/or littermates too early often fail to develop appropriate social skills, such as learning how to send and receive signals, what an 'inhibited bite' (acceptable mouthing pressure) means, and how far to go in play-wrestling," according to the Humane Society. "Play is important for kittens because it increases their physical coordination, social skills, and learning limits. By interacting with their mother and littermates, kittens explore the ranking process."

Another skill kittens that are removed from their mothers too early don't learn is one of the most basic to all felines: hunting. Although all healthy kittens show interest in predatory behavior, hunting isn't entirely instinctual. Mother cats play an important role in teaching their young to hunt by bringing them both dead prey and live prey, and allowing kittens to observe their hunting techniques. Research by biologist Robert Tabor, one of the world's leading authorities on cats, found that kittens removed from their mothers at a young age use less effective hunting techniques than those who learned to hunt alongside their mothers.

Plus, a 2017 study of nearly 6,000 cats by the University of Helsinki found that early weaning is linked to several undesirable behaviors in our feline companions, including shyness, excessive grooming, and aggression. Studies on other animal species, including rodents, monkeys, and even humans have produced similar results.

"The impacts of early weaning seem to manifest specifically as aggression and stereotypic behavior, which suggests changes in the neurotransmitters of the basal ganglia," notes Dr. Hannes Lohi, who led the study. He recommends that kittens not be weaned from their mothers until at least 14 weeks of age, describing it as "an easy and cost-efficient way of improving the quality of life of cats."

Life in a (Boring) Bubble

Whether they live in a cramped uptown apartment or a spacious country home, *felis interius* rarely ventures beyond the walls of their home except for the occasional veterinary visit or door-dashing incident. If he's lucky, the cat within these walls may encounter a catnip mouse or scratching post, but rarely will he have access to the full extent of enrichment he requires.

There's little, if anything to climb—if that's even allowed—and never anything new to explore. Cats are known for their curiosity, and if you've ever noticed your cat sniffing at your shoes when you come inside or pawing or yowling at a closed closet door, it's clear that she's intrigued by the sight, scent, or even simply the possibility of something new to investigate.

An Artificial Existence

While a window may offer a glimpse of another world, *felis interius* never actually gets to interact with that world or experience the sights, scents, and sounds of the natural world. There's no direct sunlight to bask in, no grass underfoot to roll in or chew on, no soil to dig in, no fresh air to sniff and delight in. The cat's entire world is predictable and unnatural—from the synthetic carpet fibers beneath his paws to the climate-controlled air he breathes.

Felines' senses are highly evolved and extremely sensitive, but instead of having their senses engaged by a rustle of leaves or the scent of a squirrel, cats are more likely to encounter the rustle of packaged foods or the scent of the chemicals we use to clean our homes.

Kitty Couch Potato

Cats are often characterized as lazy animals, which is no surprise, considering how often we catch our indoor cats sleeping and the widely accepted notion that felines can catnap for up to 20 hours a day. However, the truth, according to International Cat Care, is that "an active, normal cat won't sleep all of the time in the same way as it's able to do when stuck at home and given everything it needs."

All that napping, as well as the ease—and amount—of which food they eat, really adds up and contributes to indoor cats' expanding girth. In 2017, an estimated 60 percent of US cats were overweight or obese, according to the Association for Pet Obesity Prevention.

While cats in the wild eat a variety of foods and they are actively hunting and snacking in many locations throughout the day, *felis interius* will often consume the exact same highly processed food every day of her life. This food is typically left in the same location and always available, freeing up more time for cats to do nothing but nap.

Doing Business Where No One Wants to Do Business

The life of a natural outdoor cat is one of choices and preferences in all aspects of life, including when it comes to urinating and defecating. In the outdoors, a cat can select not only a location, but also a substance, whether it's grass or soil or sand.

However, *felis interius* is given no such option. This cat has only a small rectangular box and must use the type of litter his owner selects. Many cats, especially declawed ones, are sensitive to the feel of litter on their feet, and certain types of litter may not only be uncomfortable but also inherently unattractive, due to strong scents.

Location is another issue. It's not uncommon for cat owners to hide litter boxes away in basements, utility closets, and laundry rooms, which forces cats to use the bathroom in a single location that may be unappealing for a variety of reasons, including cramped space and loud, frightening sounds (like a washing machine) that may deter the cat from using the litter box. And today, with the variety of innovative ways we've found to hide litter boxes in furniture or tuck them away in cabinets, cats are often even further enclosed in small, dark, smelly spaces that we can't blame them for wanting to avoid.

Not Feeling So "Clawsome"

Felis interius can often be identified by the fact that her paws lack claws. In fact, 25–43 percent of all cats in America are declawed, a medical procedure that involves the amputation of a cat's toes, according to the Paw Project, a nonprofit that educates the public on why declawing is an inhumane procedure. Pet cats are frequently declawed simply because owners want to deter cats from the instinctual desire to scratch. This can result in lifelong pain for the cat and deter them not only from scratching, but also from playing and enjoying life.

> **"[Cats are] sort of like zoo animals— they are certainly protected generally from predation and injury and infectious disease and all of that, but they are at greater risk for diseases associated with chronic stress."**

This Life Makes Me Sick

Ironically, while many cat owners house their cats exclusively inside to keep them healthy, *felis interius* is actually more likely to suffer from a host of physical and mental health issues because of their indoor lifestyle. Due to their lack of physical activity, as well as containment in an unenriching environment, indoor cats are more likely to suffer from serious health conditions, including obesity, diabetes, and cystitis. They're also more prone to developing mental health issues, like depression, and boredom-related behavioral conditions, like aggression and elimination outside the litter box.

"A lot of veterinarians [recommend keeping cats indoors] because they are concerned about cats getting hurt and sick, but they don't think about the potential downside . . . of keeping the cat indoors," says Dr. Tony Buffington, creator of the Indoor Pet Initiative, an online resource designed to help cat owners understand feline behavior and enrich cats' lives. "It's sort of like zoo animals— they are certainly protected generally from predation and injury and infectious disease and all of that, but, like cats, they are at greater risk for diseases associated with chronic stress."

Myth: Indoor-Only Cats Live Longer

It's commonly accepted that indoor cats live longer than outdoor cats. However, studies examining this issue have compared feral cats with indoor-only cats—not indoor/outdoor cats with owners who provide food and medical care.

- Do indoor-only cats live longer than feral cats? Yes.
- Do they live longer than stray cats? Yes.
- Do they live longer than owned indoor/outdoor cats? The truth is we don't know.

No studies that we know of have looked specifically at the average life span of indoor-only cats versus owned indoor/outdoor cats that are cared for. There is, however, anecdotal evidence that they live just as long.

No Home to Call My Own

Felis interius may find himself living in a variety of places throughout his life: on the street, in various shelters and foster homes, and in numerous so-called permanent homes that may or may not actually be that long-lived. Those cats that have difficulty adjusting to indoor life or a less-than-ideal environment—caused by improper care, irresponsible pet ownership, or conflicts in multi-pet households, just to name a few—are the most likely to end up abandoned or relinquished to a shelter. And the number of cats in US shelters isn't small. The American Society for the Prevention of Cruelty to Animals estimates that 70–75 percent of the two to three million felines that enter US shelters each year are euthanized.

How We Got Here

Cats have lived outside for more than 10,000 years. In fact, they existed entirely outdoors until just about 70 years ago.

The earliest ancestors of the cats we know and love today came from southwest Asia and into Europe as early as 4400 BCE. Then, about 8,000 years ago, humans shifted from a nomadic lifestyle and established farming communities. These crops attracted mice and other rodents, which looked like good eating to the cats. So the felines moved in as well, establishing a mutually beneficial relationship with humans as mousers.

"This is probably how the first encounter between humans and cats occurred," writes Claudio Ottoni, a paleogeneticist who analyzed the DNA of more than 200 cats, including the remains of Egyptian feline mummies, told *National Geographic*. "It's not that humans took some cats and put them inside cages."

So, in a sense, cats began to domesticate themselves.

Still, they remained outdoors until a few key events occurred. One of these was the discovery of litter in 1947. "The biggest complaint about cats being solely indoors was, 'But where do they go to the bathroom?'" says certified animal behavior consultant Steve Dale. "Once kitty litter was invented, [the number of indoor cats] began to skyrocket because people who wanted to live with their cats found a practical way to do it."

The development of refrigeration and the creation of inexpensive cat food also played a role in moving cats indoors. Before this, feeding a pet cat that couldn't supplement his diet by scavenging and hunting wouldn't have been affordable for most people.

Finally, the availability of spaying and neutering was also a game changer for felines, since keeping an intact cat indoors wasn't exactly easy during mating season.

So that's what brought cats indoors, but there are several other factors that have kept them there—much more than simply the fact that they're so gosh darn cute and we desperately want to snuggle with them. But, along those lines, there's certainly something to be said about the human-animal bond.

Yes, we love our cats, and, as any good kitty caregiver knows, that love is mutual. Cats show affection toward us in a variety of ways: through purring, slow blinks, grooming us, head bunting, and just following us from room to room of the house. "If you look up the definition of 'love,' I think it's clear that cats love us just as dogs do because they have a very similar bond with people," Dale says.

Of course, when you love someone or something, you want to protect it, so that's one reason we keep our kitties locked away from the dangers of the outdoors. Because there *are* dangers: traffic, predators, and disease, just to name a few. This is why the American Veterinary Medical Association encourages cat owners to keep cats indoors. After all, the odds of our beloved pets being exposed to cars or coyotes is substantially lower inside the house. However, other dangers to our felines' physical and mental health—such as toxins, chemicals, and even other pets—do exist indoors, which we'll explore in greater detail in later chapters. And while we love our children, we don't (hopefully) confine them inside for their entire lives. Nor do we open the door and allow them to come and go as they please.

In more recent years, the effect feral and outdoor owned cats have on wildlife has also bolstered arguments to keep cats indoors. Reports issued by the American Bird Conservancy and other birding organizations claim that cats kill millions of birds each year; this has prompted salacious headlines about "killer kitties." Cats themselves are predators and are certainly responsible for the death of some birds, lizards, and other animals. But numerous scientists, researchers, and academics have concluded that the number of birds killed—whether by feral cats or owned indoor/outdoor cats—is wildly overstated. Dale, for example, acknowledges that cats do kill small wildlife. However, "the birding organizations appear to exaggerate for fund-raising purposes how many animals are actually killed by cats," he points out. We'll take a deeper look at this later in the book.

So that's how cats made the transition from outdoor mousers to indoor companions. In the roughly 8,000 years that cats have lived alongside us, it's only in the last several decades that indoor-only cats have become common. This is a minuscule amount of time on the evolutionary scale, and the genetic mapping of both wild and domestic cats reveals no major differences in their genetic makeup.

What does this mean for our house panthers? Let's take a look.

CHAPTER 2

Enclosed in Four Walls: Daily Life for *Felis Interius*

Your POV: My cat is so lucky to live this life.	Kitty POV: I didn't choose to live this way. In fact, if given the choice, I probably wouldn't.

It was once difficult to imagine what life was like for indoor cats. But that all changed with the COVID-19 pandemic.

The majority of us were confined to our homes for months at a time, and, before long, the days started to bleed together. Without the daily routine of work, school, errands, and social activities that we'd grown accustomed to, we adopted new ones as the monotony—and, for many of us, the anxiety—took hold.

It affected all of us in different ways. We might have slept later or napped more often. We might have snacked more and exercised less. We might have indulged in more Netflix, breathed less fresh air, and rarely ventured into the sun. We might have remained in our pajamas for days on end and wondered when was the last time we saw a person face-to-face.

Even the most introverted of humans are still social creatures, and being unable to live life as we normally do—unable to go places, see friends, and visit family—goes against our very nature. So it's no surprise that our physical and mental health took a serious hit during this time. Rates of depression and post-traumatic stress disorder rose, as did substance abuse. And a 2020 study published in the *Asian Journal of Psychiatry* found that stress, anxiety, loneliness, panic, fear, and difficulty concentrating all skyrocketed while our motivation dipped to an all-time low.

Those of us with children witnessed our kids struggling to adapt as well. Perhaps they even acted out, rebelling against the confinement, throwing tantrums, or simply becoming listless and lethargic.

The quarantine experience provides us with firsthand insight into the life of indoor cats. Our feline friends are essentially still wildcats with a prey drive, an instinctual desire to scratch their territory, and a need for physical activity and mental stimulation. The problem is that we've enclosed these adorable little beasts in four walls and often deny them opportunities to truly be cats. Being trapped inside, with a need to move, interact, and explore, but with few outlets to do so, takes its toll. And when cats' needs for enrichment and activity aren't met, they develop physical, mental, and behavioral problems, just as we do.

This might cause depression and anxiety. It might manifest in behaviors like house soiling, overgrooming, fearfulness, and aggression. And it might even lead to the development of serious health conditions, such as skin, gastrointestinal, and even airway diseases.

While quarantine life felt endless for many of us, we could at least find comfort in the fact that our cabin fever wouldn't last forever. But for indoor cats it does. And, too often, cats that don't adapt to indoor life easily, and don't fit our idea of what a house cat should be, are seen as disposable.

In fact, behavioral issues are the most common reason that cats are relinquished to shelters. And it's in shelters that cats are confronted with the number-one cause of death in felines in America: euthanasia. This is a form of natural selection that will only further contribute to the development of *felis interius*. After all, the cats that fall in line with people's expectations and are most successful at denying their core nature are the ones that will survive.

But this doesn't have to be the case. All indoor-only cats can thrive, but in order for us to take steps to improve their lives, first we need to fully understand their situation.

Myth: Cats Sleep All Day

Our indoor cats sleep *a lot*. They sleep on the couch, under the couch, in Amazon boxes, atop the refrigerator, in the sink, on the stairs, in the middle of the hallway, and, occasionally, even in the expensive cat beds we bought them.

It's commonly accepted that cats can sleep 16 to 20 hours per day and even spend waking hours lazing around, but this isn't true of all cats. Feral and free-roaming cats actually sleep less than this. On top of that, they're also much more active.

It's thought that feral cats hunt 10–20 times a day, but if felines sleep up to 20 hours a day, how could they possibly do this? The truth of the matter is that cats are naturally much more active than we acknowledge.

As for owned indoor/outdoor cats, many of which roam during the day and return to their indoor homes at night, they're also much more active—and adventurous—than their humans would expect. When *National Geographic* teamed up with University of Georgia researchers in 2012 to equip 55 pet cats with tiny cameras, they collected more than 2,000 hours of feline footage. So what did they find?

Although most cats don't roam too far from home, they do their fair share of exploring. The felines equipped with kitty cams "spent a lot of time under cars, inside of cars, inside of sewers, climbing roofs, climbing fences," study author Sonia Hernandez told CBS News. "I think they have intriguing lives because they do things we'd never expected them to do."

In a similar study by the University of Derby in 2019, 16 indoor/out-door cats were equipped with cameras, and Dr. Maren Huck dispelled the myth that our kitties nap as often when they're allowed access to the great outdoors. "Cats are seen as relatively lazy, especially compared to dogs," she told *Science* magazine. "But we saw that when they were outside, they became super alert."

Indoor Cats Have No Choices

Daily life for indoor-only cats is like an endless quarantine—but with far fewer choices. While being home day after day took its toll on us, at least we had opportunities to try to mix things up. We could change the TV channel, pick up a new hobby, or even decide to experiment with a new recipe for dinner. We could step outside, sit on the balcony, or go for a walk. But the limited choices we made to disrupt the monotony typically aren't extended to our feline friends.

Cats can't open a new window for something new to watch, they can't order a new toy to play with, and they can't choose what they'd like to have for dinner. They certainly can't venture outdoors to feel the sun on their fur and the wind in their whiskers. Every day, they're in the same space, eating the same food, doing the same thing they did the day before . . . and the day before that.

"When a cat is inside, nothing changes unless the human changes it for them," says Kitten Lady Hannah Shaw. "And that, I think, is the saddest thing about being a strictly indoor cat, especially if you have a human caregiver who is not really aware that you're captive. Because that's exactly what you are—captive."

> **"When a cat is inside, nothing changes unless the human changes it for them."**

Felines have no agency over their own lives, but there are numerous ways that we can provide them with more choices and more freedom so they can live better lives—even if that choice is to go outside.

"We are all different," said Dr. Buffington. "We all have preferences. And that is where choice comes in. So, to me, the optimal environment is one where the cat is allowed to choose for itself."

Indoor Cats Live in a World That Wasn't Designed for Them

When you were a child, it was obvious that much of the world wasn't made with you in mind—considering your tiny hands, your short stature, and your constant need for entertainment and enrichment.

You relied on a stool or a helping hand to reach the sink to wash your hands. You required a car seat to travel, and toys and distractions to keep you calm and entertained. And unless you visited a child-friendly location, like a park or a kids' restaurant, it was clear that most places weren't meant for children.

For an indoor cat living in our homes, the world is much like this. Whether you live in a house, an apartment, or even a van, virtually every aspect of the environment is designed for *your* ease and *your* comfort alone.

And it's not just the furniture and appliances that are made for you; it's your environment as a whole. Take temperature, for example. Odds are, you set the thermostat based on your own comfort level. However, your thermoneutral zone—the range of temperatures where your body can easily maintain its own temperature—is far different from a cat's. The thermoneutral zone for domestic cats is 86–100.4°F, but most homes where they reside are kept closer to 72°F, indicating that thermal discomfort may be common among indoor felines.

Noise and odor are other good examples of how the indoor environment can be difficult for cats to cope with. Other mammals depend on olfactory clues far more than humans do, so it's no surprise that objectionable odors—such as the scent of other pets and household cleaning agents—can be a source of chronic stress for indoor cats. And household sounds can also be difficult for felines to cope with. The auditory frequency range of cats exceeds that of humans, and research has found that cats can better thrive when the noise level is reduced to 60 decibels, the level of quiet conversation.

Plus, the unnatural environment of an indoor cat can also have negative impacts. Research shows that the number of indoor cats that develop asthma is on the rise as they're more often exposed to cigarette smoke, dust, and human dandruff.

And while we may applaud ourselves for keeping our cats safe from many of the toxic dangers of the outdoors, such as poisonous plants and antifreeze, the truth is that our homes are full of dangerous substances. From house cleaners and air fresheners to insecticides and human medications, there's an extensive list of toxins lurking in the average home. And many of them seem so innocuous that they're often left on tables and countertops, such as lilies, grapes, garlic, coffee, ribbons, thread, and candy, just to name a few.

For example, when one of Laura's cats, Travis, knocked a bottle of vitamin D supplements on the floor and tried to scarf down a pill, she learned that what's a healthy supplement for us can be deadly for a feline. So now that vitamin D is kept off the counter and inaccessible to curious cats like Travis who love to continually test gravity.

Indoor Cats Live an Unnatural, Artificial Existence

Not only is the indoor environment not designed with felines in mind, but it also defies their very nature.

As we touched on earlier, domestic cats may have lived alongside us for thousands of years, but they've only made the move inside within the last century. And even though we consider them a domesticated species, there's no denying that our felines are still genetically almost exactly like their wild ancestors.

So our house panthers are, in a sense, still actual panthers. But they walk on carpet and tile, instead of grass and dirt. They bask in the light filtered through blinds and windows, instead of direct sunlight. They hear the sound of the air-conditioning and the television, instead of the sounds of nature. And they breathe climate-controlled air, laced with our favorite fragrances, instead of the scent of fresh earth.

And while they may genetically remain essentially the same, the behavior of the indoor cat certainly points to the development of *felis interius*. Nowhere can we see this more clearly than in the sleep and activity patterns of feral and free-roaming cats as opposed to indoor ones.

Cats without homes engage in "high activity" 14 percent of the time, compared with only 3 percent for indoor cats, according to a University of Illinois study. It's not a surprising finding, given that feral cats are responsible for their own meals. "The unowned cats have to find food to survive, and their activity is significantly greater than the owned cats throughout the day and through the year, especially in winter," according to study coauthor Jeff Horn.

So What's the Solution?

How do you allow your indoor cat to tap into his natural instincts and live a more fulfilling life? Throw away the kibble, open the front door, and let your cat fend for himself? Not quite. Actually, *please* don't do that.

"You don't have to import mice into your house for a cat to be happy," Dale says. "But we can find ways to enrich cats' environments to keep them happy."

We can start simply by doing what you're doing right now: understanding the predicament your indoor cat is in. "The reality is that we just need to look at the world through cats' eyes and think like a cat and be a cat for a moment or two, so we can make life better for them," says Becky Robinson, president and founder of the feline advocacy organization Alley Cat Allies.

Understanding leads to empathy, and that sparks change. And you can begin right now by making small environmental changes and providing opportunities for your cat to do a little something new. And don't worry: It's not going to break the bank.

> "We just need to look at the world through cats' eyes and think like a cat and be a cat for a moment or two, so we can make life better for them."

"The most important thing to know is it doesn't have to be expensive to have enrichment in your home," Kitten Lady Hannah Shaw observes. "I always feel a little discouraged when people write off enrichment because they think it involves a trip to the pet supply store and that if they can't afford to fill their cart with stuff, then they can't do enrichment in the home. Because we all know some of the best enrichment is free things like cardboard boxes and packing paper."

Throughout this book, we'll provide you with a multitude of enrichment ideas for your feline friend. But while we'd love you to read this book from cover to cover, it's a great idea to "paws," grab a bookmark, and begin implementing some of these changes. Here's a great way to get started: Simply come up with ways to make your cat's life a tiny bit different each day. In other words, break your indoor kitty out of the monotony of quarantine life!

"Pawsome" Ways to Vary Daily Life for Indoor Cats

- Open a screened-in window.
- Create food-foraging opportunities. (More on this in chapter 6.)
- Rotate toys so what's old is new again.
- Put a favorite toy in a challenging place, such as in a shoe, under a blanket, etc.
- Build a fort from boxes, blankets, pillows, and couch cushions. (Children aren't the only ones who enjoy this.)
- Create a window seat or perch.
- Crack open a closet door.
- Chase an ice cube in an empty bathtub.
- Do some clicker training.
- Bring a piece of the outdoors in for kitty to investigate, such as a branch or a leaf.
- Rearrange a room.
- Toss packing paper or tissue paper on the floor, and let kitty play with it and shred it.
- Grow indoor grass.
- Introduce a new object to chase, such as a wine cork, a bottle cap, a toilet paper roll, a ball of tinfoil, etc.
- Put on a YouTube video of birds and squirrels.

- Fill a tub or a children's pool with an inch or two of water and drop in ping-pong balls, corks, and other floating toys.
- Leave a new, empty box out or move a box to a new location.
- Shove a bit of tissue paper and catnip or silver vine (another olfactory stimulant that can also bring on a euphoric state) into a toilet paper roll and let your kitty shred it.
- Offer scent-enrichment opportunities—and not just catnip. Let kitty sniff what you're cooking, the package that just arrived, etc.

CHAPTER 3

The Bathroom "Purroblem"

Your POV:
All I need to do is provide a litter box and clean it occasionally.

Kitty POV:
What if you could use only public restrooms?

The litter box is an essential part of indoor cat life. And litter box issues—namely, cats choosing to do their business outside the box—are one of the most common complaints that kitty caregivers have. In fact, inappropriate elimination is responsible for up to half the complaints about feline behavior, according to a University of Pennsylvania study, and it's the most common behavior for which people relinquish their cats to shelters. At least 10 percent of indoor cats develop elimination problems, according to the American Society for the Prevention of Cruelty to Animals.

The discovery that your precious little fur baby has been spraying or choosing to use the carpet, your houseplants, or even your bed as his new bathroom is hardly a pleasant one. But too often cat owners react with anger, as if their cat had soiled their favorite sweater as an act of vengeance. Or, they bring their pet back to the scene of the crime and attempt to scold him with firm "no" or "bad boy," as if this would deter their cat from doing it again. (Spoiler alert: It won't.)

To solve litter box problems, we must first attempt to understand *why* our cats are thinking—and going—outside the litter box. And, often, your cat is seeking an alternative toilet for the exact same reason you would.

When you enter a public restroom and discover that the stall's previous occupant failed to flush, you very likely move on to the next stall. When given the choice between a restroom and a porta-potty, odds are, you'll choose to forgo the stuffy, enclosed box that's been baking in the sun all day. Of course, we'll use these less-than-ideal bathrooms if we must. But if there's an alternative, we'll take it. Cats are no different.

Yet we expect our feline friends to essentially use public restrooms and porta-potties on a daily basis. Even if a multi-cat home has more than one litter box, cats are forced to urinate and defecate where someone else already has. In other words, it's an unflushed toilet. And while cats might prefer a bit of space to do their business, they're often forced into an enclosed box, trapping them inside, along with the very odors we ourselves would like to avoid. In other words, it's a porta-potty that cats must venture into several times a day.

Considering the litter box from this point of view, can you blame your cat for seeking an alternative? Wouldn't you?

And just because your cat isn't going outside the litter box doesn't necessarily mean she's satisfied with her box. A 2017 study, published in *Applied Animal Behaviour Science*, compared how cats used both "enriched environments" (large boxes filled with loose, sandy, scooping litter) and "clinical environments" (small commercial boxes containing polypropylene beans instead of litter). The researchers found that cats will often continue to use a box even when their behavior in and around the box indicates frustration.

The most pronounced differences in behavior between the two environments occurred post-elimination, or after cats had urinated or defecated. After completing their business, cats spent significantly more time in the less-appealing box—often up to two minutes. Why? Often because these spaces required them to expend additional effort scratching in, on, and around the box in an attempt to cover their excrement.

This covering behavior is thought to be a way for cats to cover their scent, both reducing exposure to pathogens and preventing predators from detecting the cat's presence. While indoor cats certainly don't need to worry about a predator stumbling upon their litter box, the motivation to engage in this behavior remains. Being unable to cover excrement optimally can cause frustration for the cat. So it's likely that cats' repetitive pawing behavior post-elimination is a manifestation of this stress.

However, cats may also reveal that they're unhappy with the state of their box during elimination. They may appear restless, walking and shifting often, or even balancing on the side of the box.

Further, the study found that cats using the less desirable boxes urinated less often and for longer than those with the preferable environment, indicating that they're holding their urine. Indoor cats are already prone to urinary issues, so this behavior could have serious medical implications. Just as holding urine for long durations can be detrimental to humans, the same may be true for cats.

If your cat exhibits any of the following behaviors, she may be communicating that her litter box experience is unacceptable:

- Hesitating when entering the box
- Entering and exiting the litter box before eliminating
- Balancing on the side of the box
- Post-elimination scratching at the side of the litter box or "box banging" in covered boxes
- Post-elimination scratching outside the litter box, such as on the floor or on the wall
- Raising a paw on the side of the litter box while eliminating
- Keeping the head outside a covered litter box while eliminating
- Using the litter box less often and eliminating for longer periods of time

Clearly, there are numerous reasons that cats may be unhappy with their litter boxes, even bypassing them entirely and doing their business elsewhere. Let's take a look at these in greater detail, so you can not only understand the feline perspective, but also learn how to overcome the problem and find a solution that doesn't stink for you or your cat.

Cleanliness

When cat owners come to a veterinarian or feline behaviorist with complaints that their pet isn't using the litter box, often the first question the professionals will ask is this: "How frequently are you cleaning the box?" And all too often the response is "weekly" or "every few days."

What if that's how often you were permitted to flush the toilet? Sounds like a crappy situation, right? You deserve better than that, and so does your cat. Felines don't want to walk across areas that have been urinated or defecated on, so they'll avoid these like land mines . . . and may forgo the litter box altogether.

The solution is simple: "Flush the toilet," aka "scoop the litter," more often—ideally, several times a day. Cats use the litter box three to five times throughout the day, and in a multi-cat household, all that waste can quickly add up.

Remember: If you're going to keep your cat inside, provide him with what he'd seek outside—an unsoiled space to do his business. In the outdoors, cats urinate in new clean spots all the time, so if we want them go in the same spot each time, we have to keep it clean . . . or else.

Odor

When it comes to litter box smells, we're referring to more than just the unpleasant odors your cat creates himself. Scented litter, air fresheners, and deodorizers are often used in and around litter boxes, and while these fragrances may be pleasing to you, your cat may feel differently.

Studies of whether cats prefer scented or unscented litter have had somewhat mixed results. A 1997 study, published in *Applied Animal Behaviour Science*, revealed a correlation between the use of scented litter and litter box problems, while a 2011 study by Dr. Jacqueline Neilson found that cats used unscented litter only slightly more often than scented.

Further research shows that the scent of litter, or the scents used around the box from air fresheners, for example, may be more indicative of feline preference. Cats tend to prefer the scent of cedar, but avoid citrus and floral scents. So the question might be less about whether scented litter or air fresheners should be used and more a question of *what kind of scents* are present.

If your cat is exhibiting frustrated litter box behavior or avoiding the box entirely, consider what smells your pet may be encountering. Your cat has 200 million scent receptors (you have a mere 56 million), so when it comes to litter box odor, your cat is having a much more intense sensory experience than you are. This is why feline behaviorist Jackson Galaxy writes, "I recommend only unscented litter, with none of those perfumed, sprinkle-in-the-box powders

and no air fresheners (plug-in or otherwise) right next to the box. In my experience, those strong, artificial fragrances, including scented litter, can drive your cat away."

Kitty Care: How Many Litter Boxes Do You Need?

You've likely heard that you need one litter box per cat or even 1½ litter boxes per cat. These are good rules of thumb, but there's no hard-and-fast rule that dictates how many are required.

It actually depends on several factors: how clean the boxes are, where they're located, your cats' preferences, and more. For example, one box in a single-cat home is just fine as long as it's kept clean. And a couple of litter boxes that are scooped several times a day may work for two to three felines in the same home.

But, ideally, have as many litter boxes in the home as you can accommodate. The idea is to make it easy for cats to find a clean box when they need it, rather than forcing them to use the same dirty one again and again.

Also, keep in mind that cats are a lot like us. Sure, we'd prefer to have our own bathroom, but we're often forced to share, and this can work just fine, as long as the person we're sharing with is respectful and compatible.

Size and Location

Most litter boxes are made with human convenience in mind. They're small and designed to be easily tucked into corners. And, these days, cat owners have come up with a variety of creative ways to hide litter boxes. From benches, cupboards, and trunks designed to contain the box, to "IKEA hacks" that enable us to conceal it entirely, there's no shortage of ways to seemingly make the litter box disappear.

Again, the problem with these solutions is that they're solutions for people—not cats. What if you had to crawl inside a cramped dark space every time you needed to use the bathroom? Wouldn't you seek an alternative?

"Bathrooms, mudrooms, and garages are not places that a cat finds to be territorially valuable, even when a litter box is placed there," says feline behaviorist Daniel Quagliozzi. "I recommend multiple choice open and uncovered litter boxes, situated in rooms of the highest social importance, like living rooms, home offices, and bedrooms with clear vantage points in all directions to eliminate insecurity or fear."

In the same 2017 study on litter box usage, the researchers found that, regardless of whether cats used the preferable box or the less preferable one, the animals utilized the entire space available to them. This indicates that cats may have a preference for larger litter boxes, which allow them to more easily engage in elimination behaviors necessary for their physical and mental well-being. In fact, the study concludes that "size should be

considered more strongly when designing litter boxes, taking into account the cat's perspective."

If they were outside, cats would have the entire world to use as their litter box. But, indoors, we expect them to eliminate in the same place all the time.

The solution? When it comes to litter boxes, bigger is better. Sure, the box may not fit as easily into a closet, but wouldn't you also prefer not to use the toilet inside a closet?

If they were outside, cats would have the entire world to use as their litter box. But, indoors, we expect them to eliminate in the same place all the time. The very least we can do is give them a bit more space.

And while we require privacy and a closed door when we're in the bathroom, cats actually feel safer if they have a clear vantage

Myth: Only Destructive Cats Eliminate outside the Litter Box

When a cat isn't using the litter box, owners may be quick to assume that a cat is simply being vindictive or intentionally destructive. However, cats may quit using their box for a variety of reasons that have nothing to do with getting back at you for not sharing your tuna sandwich. Oftentimes, cats are simply reacting to the space you've created for them, so it's up to you to create a more inviting litter box environment.

point and multiple ways to access and escape their litter box. In the wild, cats are understandably vulnerable when they relieve themselves, so they keep an eye on their surroundings and know their escape routes. It makes sense then that cats in an enclosed litter box or a tiny room with only one exit might feel uneasy when they enter a confined space where they can't see potential threats or make an easy getaway.

Stress and Fear

What if every time you needed to use the bathroom, you had to fight your way past your obnoxious older brother? What if every other time you entered the bathroom, a scary, unexplainable noise erupted out of nowhere? Now a necessary part of your daily routine is accompanied by frustration, anxiety, or even outright fear. This is often the case with indoor cats.

There are numerous reasons why cats may begin to associate their litter boxes with stress. For example, in multi-cat homes, there may be inter-cat issues, such as resource guarding, where one cat tries to prevent another from using it. Or a cat may have a negative or fearful experience in the litter box, which could encompass anything from being chased away from the box by a dog to simply hearing frightening sounds because the box is shoved into a closet next to the water heater. Moving to a new home, the arrival of a new family member, or the introduction of a new pet may also cause stress that results in elimination outside the litter box.

While some of these stressors are unavoidable, others can be easily resolved by simply providing multiple litter boxes and placing them in quieter, more appealing areas.

Medical Conditions

Many cats may simply exhibit litter box problems for health reasons, and any cat going outside the box should be seen by a veterinarian.

Senior cats may develop arthritis that makes it difficult to enter top-entry boxes or boxes with higher walls. Felines may also have a medical condition that makes urination painful. In these cases, they may avoid the litter box because it's where they associate experiencing this pain, or they may simply have to urinate with such urgency that they can't make it to the litter box in time.

Urinary tract infections, feline interstitial cystitis, bladder stones, and blockages can all occur in cats, and, oftentimes, stress can cause or exacerbate conditions like cystitis. These medical conditions can be fatal if left untreated, so it's important for cat owners to keep a close eye on their pets' litter box behaviors.

Cats suffering from diabetes or kidney disease may drink a lot of water and use the box in great volume at one time or even hold urine in for a long time and urinate a lot. When this occurs, the urine soaks the litter around their feet, causing it to clump and stick to their paws. Lynn has seen numerous felines with soiled

Do This, Not That

DO try to get to the root of the problem. Assess your cat's behavior, see how she interacts with the litter box, and look for solutions. You may want to consult your vet or a certified feline behaviorist.

DON'T punish your cat for going outside the litter box. Cats don't learn from negative reinforcement, so this would likely backfire, causing additional fear and stress that might only exacerbate the problem, as well as hurt your relationship with your cat.

litter stuck in the pads of their feet or even forming cement-like blocks on their paws, a condition she calls white-paw syndrome. If you notice this occurring on your cat's feet, seek veterinary help immediately.

And, finally, declawed cats are also prone to litter box issues because they're so often in lifelong pain. More on this later.

Preferences

Finally, cats may be frustrated with their bathroom situation simply because something about their experience isn't working for them. Just as you may prefer to visit a particular bathroom in the house or use a certain type of toilet paper, your cat may also have preferences. However, it's impossible for cats to communicate these predilections because they've likely never been given the opportunity to make a choice.

Feral and free-roaming cats can decide where they urinate and defecate, but indoor cats are simply stuck with whatever we give them. Today, litter is available in a variety of materials that have unique scents and textures, and while one cat may prefer wheat litter, another may prefer paper.

How much litter is in a box may also deter or attract a cat. Felines scratch in their litter, so they need an adequate amount in order to engage in this behavior. Pam Johnson-Bennett, who's authored several books on cat behavior, recommends that owners maintain three to four inches of litter, but you may find that your individual kitty prefers more or less. For example, when Quagliozzi recently worked with a cat that was eliminating outside the box, he recommended "a shallow litter depth of an inch to mimic the preference of eliminating on hard or shallow absorbent places."

There's also the type of litter box to consider. While some cats may be comfortable disappearing into a covered box for a little privacy, others may feel cramped or trapped and prefer a more open space. Top-entry litter boxes are popular choices for cat owners whose felines scatter litter throughout the house, but some cats may simply not like these and choose to avoid them entirely. The key here is to provide your cat with options.

Plus, the type of box your cat needs may change as he ages. Kittens need shallower boxes that are easier to enter, and senior cats and those with arthritis often need the same kind of design. Senior cats may also require a ramp to get into and out of the box and may not be comfortable with a top-entry box.

CHAPTER 4

You're Not Getting the "Meowsage"

Your POV: I want you to stop scratching!	Kitty POV: But this is how I communicate.

When you first wake up in the morning, or when you rise from a well-deserved afternoon nap, you likely stretch. You extend your arms and legs, curl your toes, turn your head from side to side to work out a crick in your neck. You likely don't even think about what you're doing. It just happens. It feels good. You might even say it's instinctive.

When you're in a crowded theater and want to save a seat for a friend, you might leave your jacket or purse on the seat next to yours, wordlessly communicating that this space is taken. You don't have to inform everyone who passes by that you've reserving that seat; the message is clear.

And when you need to share news with a loved one or send a document to a coworker, you don't hesitate to pick up the phone or send an email. At our core, humans are intrinsically and biologically social creatures, so our need to communicate is one of our deepest compulsions.

In all these scenarios, we're acting with little to no thought as to what we're doing. We wake up, we stretch. We need to tell a friend that we're running 10 minutes late, we send a text. This, essentially, is what cats do when they scratch.

Now, cats scratch for a variety of reasons: to mark their territory by leaving both a visual mark and a scent (cats have scent glands in their paws), to remove the dead outer layer of their claws, to stretch and flex their muscles, and to expend energy. Plus, it simply feels nice for the cat, just as a good stretch does for you.

"Put your hand on your cat's back when they are stretching and scratching on a tall, sturdy scratching post," suggests Lori Shepler, founder of the anti-declawing nonprofit City the Kitty. "You can feel the power going through their muscles and you can tell how good it feels to them."

And scratching isn't just about claws—even declawed cats retain the instinct to scratch.

So if your cat were able to explain, step-by-step, *why* she's scratching the corner of your expensive new couch, she would probably say something like this:

"I'm so stiff from my eleventh nap of the day. Time to work the kinks out!"

"This is my territory and I love it here, so I'm going to let everyone know that this room belongs to Fluffy. No other cats need apply."

"Oh, my human is home, and I'm just so excited that I need to release this energy somehow."

In none of these scenarios does your cat intend to destroy your couch. Your kitty probably *likes* the couch. After all, it's where you snuggle up to watch TV and Fluffy gets that sweet spot behind her ears scratched. Plus, your cat may be scratching an area simply because it's where his favorite person spends time. "Cats often scratch where their beloved humans sit because they are marking

you as their territory," says veterinarian Dr. Jennifer Conrad, founder and director of the Paw Project, an organization that educates the public about declawing. "It is out of love, not spite. The message is clear: 'Hey, other cats, this is my human so move along!'"

Now that you understand why your cat is scratching, it's probably pretty clear that you can't just expect her to stop the behavior entirely. That would be like expecting you not to stretch first thing in the morning or not to call your mom or text your friends. That's a pretty absurd ask, right?

However, it seems fair to set a few ground rules. For example, you (probably) don't violently throw your arms out each morning and risk giving your partner a nosebleed. You (hopefully) don't attempt to reserve an entire row for your friends at the theater. And you don't call your best friend for a chat in the middle of that movie. You've likely learned to be somewhat civilized about these things. And when it comes to scratching, your cat can, too.

Clearly, we can't get our cats to stop scratching. So instead, we must provide them with opportunities to scratch—ones that both you and your cat can live with.

Truth: There's No Such Thing as Inappropriate Scratching

Scratching is an inherent, natural, and necessary behavior for all felines, so there's no such thing as inappropriate scratching. For a cat, it's always appropriate to scratch—as long as no one's getting hurt, of course.

Perhaps you've tried this before. You've bought expensive, carpeted scratching posts or picked up those slabs of corrugated cardboard, and, still, Fluffy opts to scratch the corner of the couch. What's up with that? Often, it comes down to preferences—and an indoor cat's lack of them. "It's rare for a cat to scratch on furniture and rugs if you provide them with appropriate scratching items," Shepler says.

To find a scratching area that your cat will actually use, instead of the couch, the carpet, or the speakers, take the following two questions into account.

Where Does Your Cat Like to Scratch?

As we said before, one of the primary reasons cats scratch is to leave both visual and scent marks that define their territory. "Pheromones are very important," says veterinary behavior expert Carlo Siracusa, animal ethics and welfare professor at the University of Pennsylvania. "Also, [scratching] leave[s] visual signs. The scratching of a cat is a visual sign to leave a message for someone who didn't find [the cat] but will find the scratch."

In other words, scratching is basically Fluffy's way of saying, "I was here," much like the way you used to carve your name into your sixth-grade desk. (You weren't being destructive. You were leaving a record for posterity!)

While cats may scratch in a variety of locations, they tend to select a small number of conspicuous objects in their environment to scratch, such as trees, fence posts, or the corner of the couch, and return to them repeatedly, often taking the same routes. It's sort of like how Hansel and Gretel left a trail of breadcrumbs to try to find their way back home, except cats mark their routes with

their claws. Felines frequently like to scratch near their favorite sleeping areas, so they can get a good stretch in after a nap. They're also often fans of scratching in or near room entrances to communicate their presence. (If your doorframes look anything like Laura's, you know this is true.) So it's a good idea to put a scratcher near doorways, so your cat can make his presence known as he enters and exits. Placing a tall post with a perch, or a cat tree, by a window is another excellent idea because it's a natural place for your feline friend to notify others of his presence. And cats also like to scratch where *you* are.

> **Your cat may be scratching an area simply because it's where his favorite person spends time.**

"Cat scratching posts and cat trees have to be where you and your family are," Dr. Conrad points out. "Remember the cat is telling other cats that you and your home are owned. So it does no good to put the post in the garage, behind the dryer, because no one is hanging out there."

You may also know other places your cat loves to scratch, such as that aforementioned couch corner or the living room rug. These are all ideal locations to place scratching posts and mats because your cat has already expressed an interest in them and developed a habit of scratching there.

If you have multiple cats, it's also a good idea to introduce scratching opportunities in areas throughout the home where cats tend to congregate. This may be near a favorite napping area, beside the litter box, by the food bowl or water fountain, or along routes to these locations.

By providing an ideal place to scratch in the areas your cat frequents and enjoys a good scratch, you're making it easy for Fluffy to opt for the post over the sofa.

What Does Your Cat Like to Scratch?

There's an abundance of scratching apparatuses on the market. From carpeted, freestanding posts and wall-mounted scratchers to cardboard mats and natural wood, there's something for every cat.

Not sure what your cat would prefer? Provide a variety of options and let him choose. Also, think about where he already scratches.

Cats with a propensity for scratching chair legs or the side of the couch or recliner may prefer a vertical scratching post, while cats that are drawn to carpets and rugs may like a horizontal one. If your cat scratches both, give him what he craves and provide both vertical and horizontal scratching opportunities.

The scratching material your cat enjoys should also be taken into account. If your cat has an inclination toward a certain material, such as carpeting, select a scratching post with a similar texture. Not sure about kitty's preferences? Again, give him options. Most cats prefer scratching areas to be made out of rough material that they can satisfyingly shred, such as sisal, cardboard, or carpeting.

Make sure the scratcher you provide is large enough for a gratifying scratch. This means vertical posts that are tall enough to provide a decent stretch and sturdy enough not to tip over during use. Also, a cat that scratches horizontally may desire a space long and wide enough for her to place her entire body atop it. "Each should be sturdy, broad-based, and at least 1½ times longer/taller than the out-stretched cat," Dr. Conrad notes.

Do This, Not That

DO provide multiple scratching opportunities.

DON'T assume that one post or scratcher is sufficient.

DO invest in quality posts that'll last a long time.

DON'T expect your cat to use flimsy or too-small scratchers that don't fulfill her scratching needs.

DO try different substrates, like cardboard, carpet, sisal rope, and more.

DON'T buy scratchers that are all of the same material.

DO use sticky tape on new furniture to discourage scratching.

DON'T bring new furniture into your home without safeguarding it first.

You can also pull double duty by purchasing or building a cat tree that cats can both climb and scratch. "Some scratching posts can also be tall cat trees," Dr. Conrad adds. "Cats prefer to surveil their territory from above, so these serve a dual purpose. Cat trees help cats feel more secure because they provide them with a place to escape from being vulnerable on the ground. Cat trees have to be sturdy and provide safe and comfortable places for the cats to sleep."

So make sure that when you provide your kitty with the scratching options he requires, you're fulfilling all his needs. That way he won't need to seek out somewhere else in your home to satisfy that desire. And keep in mind that, just like us, cats can get tired of the same old thing, so every now and then give them a new scratching opportunity.

You can even offer items to scratch that aren't exclusively manufactured and marketed for cats. Visit a thrift store and pick up an old rug or another piece of furniture that your pet can scratch to her heart's content. That's what Lynn did when her cats took an interest in the new couch. She picked up a $40 ottoman and placed it on the side of the couch where the cats were scratching. Now, Dezi and Roo scratch their very own piece of furniture and leave the couch alone. You can also purchase a strip of carpet and install it in an area just for your cat or get creative and wrap sisal rope around a staircase bannister, for example.

What about Declawed Cats?

Declawing a cat is never a humane solution to preventing a cat from scratching. As we've said, cats have a natural need to scratch, so they're going to indulge in this behavior whether they have claws or not. After all, while they may not have claws to shred, they still have scent glands and the instinct to mark their territory.

Cats without claws may still "use" regular scratching mats and posts, but others may prefer a softer material. Because every cat needs vertical space (more on that later), a cat tree covered in a variety of materials—sisal rope and soft carpeting, for example—may fit the bill. However, it's important to keep in mind that cats without claws can't climb or keep their balance as well as their nonmutilated brethren, so look for a cat tree or cat condo with numerous levels that aren't a great distance apart. This will allow your kitty to easily access every part of it and truly make it her own.

How to Get Your Kitty to Use the Scratching Post

Your cat may automatically begin to scratch on the substitute objects you've provided, but here are some steps to take to ensure that kitty is using the post instead of the couch.

First, place the scratching alternative near the object you want your cat to stop scratching. You can also cover the object or area you don't want your cat to scratch with an unpleasant material, such as aluminum foil, double-sided tape, or a plastic carpet runner with the pointy side facing out.

Help lure your cat to the preferred scratching object by sprinkling it with an irresistible scent, like catnip or silver vine. Place a favorite treat or toy on the scratcher, or engage your cat in play with a wand toy. Trail it up the side of the scratching post and create a game that invites your cat to mimic the motion of scratching.

If this is ineffective, you can also try spraying an odor your cat doesn't like, such as a citrus or menthol scent, onto the item you don't want scratched. There are also commercial sprays available that deter scratching. In areas with nonfabric surfaces, the Humane Society suggests dipping cotton balls in these scents and placing them beside the object you don't want scratched. However, use caution with odors. You don't want to deter your cat from using the scratching post or a nearby item like the litter box.

It's also important to use positive reinforcement to reward your cat for scratching in the appropriate place. When kitty scratches in the preferred location, give her praise and loving pats. You can also give her a tasty treat. But remember that timing is important. To help your cat make positive associations with scratching the desired object, reward her *while* she's performing the action. Waiting until after she's done can make it difficult for your cat to discern what she's being rewarded for.

"Cats have to be taught which places are appropriate to scratch and which places are not," Dr. Conrad points out. "Encouraging a cat to scratch on a scratching post or pad with positive rewards like petting the cat, playing with the cat, or giving a treat to the cat can reinforce the learning so the cat gets it right all the time."

However, skip the spray bottles, and never yell at a cat for scratching in the wrong place. "They won't understand what they did to deserve it and it might make them afraid of you or your voice," Dr. Conrad says. "Squirt bottles and jars of coins that make noise can just add to the cat's anxiety and be very counterproductive in teaching a cat. It is hard for anyone to learn and retain the knowledge in fearful conditions."

If, for some reason, your cat still isn't using the scratcher, consider whether the material or the placement of the scratcher is ideal. You may need to make some changes or adjustments.

Timing is important. Reward your cat *while* she's performing the preferred action. Waiting until after she's done can make it difficult for your cat to discern what she's being rewarded for.

Make Nail Trimming a Regular Practice

We've established that we can't—and shouldn't—prevent cats from scratching. However, you can trim your cat's claws so they're not so sharp.

It's easiest to get your cat used to nail trimming when she's a kitten. Simply handle the kitten's paws regularly and press gently on her paw pads to extend the claws. However, older cats can be taught to accept nail trimming as well. The trick is to go slowly. If you've never trimmed your cat's claws before, don't try to wrestle her into submission and start trimming. This won't go well for either of you.

Cats' paws are one of the most sensitive parts of their body, so if your kitty isn't used to having his feet handled, don't be surprised if he pulls away or gives you a nip. After all, this is new territory for both of you. (What if someone suddenly grabbed your feet and started touching your toes? Odds are, you'd jerk away, too.) Just as with a kitten, you want to slowly get your cat comfortable with the

Myth: Cats That Scratch Are Being Destructive

It's not about destruction. Cats scratch to communicate, mark territory, stretch, and remove the outer layer of their claws. If you don't provide them with appropriate objects to scratch, they'll find their own—and it just may be your favorite armchair.

experience of having his feet handled. So do this for a minute during a petting session, gently press the paw pads, and praise your kitty.

Once your cat is accustomed to this touching, clip that first claw with a nail clipper designed for cats—but trim just the very tip of it. When a cats' nails are extended, you can see the sharp, clear part at the tip. This is the part you want to trim. Don't cut into the pink or the darker part. This is the quick of the nail, and it'll cause pain and bleeding if it's harmed. It'll also immediately derail your nail-trimming session.

If you've never trimmed a cat's nails before, ask a veterinarian or groomer to show you how it's done. Then, make nail trimming a regular part of your cat's routine every two to three weeks.

CHAPTER 5

Paws Need Claws

Your POV: Declawing my cat is the only way to protect myself and my furniture.	Kitty POV: What if the tips of your fingers were removed?

Declawing is often compared to a fingernail trim. However, declawing, or onychectomy, isn't the equivalent of a permanent manicure. It entails multiple amputations, comparable to the removal of your fingertips at the first knuckle. In other words, imagine having all of your fingertips removed. Pretty horrific, right?

That's why veterinarian Dr. Robin Downing, director of the Downing Center for Animal Pain Management, says it's essential to call the procedure what it really is: feline toe amputation. "Why is the terminology important? Because we veterinarians have sanitized this mutilating surgery with the term *declaw*, which does not communicate what is involved, and that leaves unsuspecting cat owners ignorant of just what that term really means," Dr. Downing points out.

Again, consider undergoing a fingertip-removal procedure yourself. Even if you were under anesthesia during the actual procedure, imagine the pain you'd be in when the anesthesia wore off. Think

about all the daily tasks you'd struggle to do: picking up objects, opening doors, texting friends, making meals, typing on your computer, grasping a pencil, holding hands with a loved one. The list is endless because your fingers are an integral part of your life. They're essential to your very survival.

Of course, you'd very likely learn to adapt. People with arthritis, carpal tunnel syndrome, and other disorders acclimate. Even amputees who've lost entire limbs find ways to thrive and accomplish remarkable feats. Both humans and felines are undeniably resilient; however, just because we *can* overcome doesn't mean it's acceptable to introduce a handicap to someone. Would you wish a life of pain and struggle for your child, a friend, or even a complete stranger? Hopefully not. So, why then are an estimated 25 percent of North American cats subjected to this irreparable horror?

"Feline toe amputation can be traced back to the time when it became popular to bring cats indoors as pets, changing their role from mouser to companion," Dr. Downing notes. "The natural and

normal cat behavior of scratching on surfaces to 'mark' them with their foot pheromones was deemed inappropriate by cat owners, and veterinarians stepped up to provide a 'solution': Amputate the last bone of each toe and eliminate the problem. The procedure was marketed as an easy fix, and something that cats wouldn't mind. The thinking was that, when kittens underwent their [desexing] surgeries, they could have their toe amputations done at the same time, and they would never miss their claws. Because this combination procedure was provided by veterinarians—the supposed experts—it was accepted by unknowing cat owners. In retrospect this was clearly not veterinary medicine's finest hour."

So the surgery typically occurs because cat owners want to prevent their pets from causing damage by scratching. In fact, it may even be seen as beneficial for the cat—at least from a human perspective—because scratching is often the reason why cats are rehomed, abandoned, or relinquished to shelters.

Ironically, though, cat owners seeking to stop their felines' unwanted scratching behavior through declawing actually increase the chances that their cats will engage in other problematic behaviors. Declawing puts cats at risk of long-term pain, which often manifests as aggression, biting, and soiling outside the litter box, according to research published in the *Journal of Feline Medicine and Surgery*. Why? Because litter can be irritating to declawed paws, especially large hard pellets. But to an uncomfortable cat, the pain associated with the litter box may deter them from using it at all. And without claws as a defense mechanism, many felines turn to biting. This isn't only detrimental to the cat, who's living in pain, but also to the human–animal bond and even to human health, since cat bites can be a serious medical issue.

"Feline toe amputation involves cutting nerves to the toes, as well as the nerves in the sensitive joint capsule," Dr. Downing explains. "This creates an acute pain issue at the time of surgery and a great likelihood of ongoing, unrelenting, nerve-related pain. Post-amputation pain is a terrible problem in the human medical world, and we humans can *talk* about our pain. Cats are hardwired as we are, so their nerves experience trauma as ours do. That said, cats also do their best to hide their pain. That means we cannot really know the kind of pain and discomfort they feel in the wake of toe amputation. That chronic, maladaptive, neuropathic pain can precipitate abnormal and unacceptable behaviors, like increased willingness to bite, abnormal gait, difficulty jumping onto or off cat furniture, or inappropriate elimination due to avoiding the texture of cat litter."

Call the procedure what it really is: feline toe amputation.

Plus, as we know, these unwanted behaviors make it more likely that the cat will be abandoned or relinquished to a shelter where he'll face a high likelihood of euthanasia.

"Declawed cats are at high risk of losing their homes," Dr. Conrad says. "You can imagine that if someone was so intolerant of a cat scratching the couch, that same person is going to be really intolerant of the cat biting and not using the box. This is the reason that most reputable animal adoption places have a strict no-declaw policy. They know that if the cat gets declawed, there is a good chance that the cat is going to lose its home and that the cat will be very hard to find a new home for when they have to disclose that the cat is a biter and doesn't use the litter box."

Still, even a lack of claws won't deter a cat from scratching. This is an innate behavior that felines will engage in regardless of whether they have claws. Their desire to scratch doesn't decrease just because they've been declawed. As we explained in the previous chapter, it's instinctive for cats to mark their territory and communicate with other animals through scratching. So if a declawed cat does scratch less after amputation, this is likely due to pain.

The procedure itself—which involves the removal of not just claws, but also bones—is painful. But this pain isn't short-lived. A declawed feline can experience lifelong discomfort from infection, inflammation, and even neuropathic phantom pain, just like human amputees.

What makes matters worse is that it can be difficult for cat owners to even recognize that their pets are in pain. Take a look at just a few of the many indicators that a feline may be in pain:

- Body tension
- Flinching
- Inappropriate elimination
- Reluctance to move or put weight on the declawed limb
- Excessive grooming
- Limping
- Hiding
- Lack of interaction
- No desire to play
- Aggression

Felines exhibit pain in a variety of ways, so even if a declawed cat doesn't display any of the aforementioned behaviors, it doesn't necessarily mean that the animal isn't experiencing discomfort. "Since cats are stoic, owners will think that their declawed cats are just fine, but this is far from the truth," notes Lori Shepler. "It would be wrong to think that cats who had 10 or 20 of their toe bones amputated and have to walk on those amputation sites for the rest of their lives would be okay."

Plus, studies have found that declawed cats are more likely to develop back pain. And if their surgery isn't done well, small bone fragments can be left behind, causing even more severe pain. "They simply cannot step onto their own feet without suffering," Dr. Downing observes.

For all the reasons outlined above, it's not surprising that declawing is considered unethical—and has even been outlawed—in

"More caring veterinarians are realizing that declawing has no benefit whatsoever . . . After all, veterinarians went to school to protect cats, not couches!"

numerous countries for any reason other than a medical condition, such as cancer. More than 40 countries, including England, France, Germany, Israel, and New Zealand have made declawing illegal. And it's outlawed in several US cities and the entire state of New York. Plus a number of other states have introduced legislation to ban it.

"In 2020, the two largest veterinary chain hospitals, VCA and Banfield, stopped declawing in all of their 2,000-plus hospitals," Dr. Conrad says. "The industry is changing and more and more caring veterinarians are realizing that declawing has no benefit whatsoever to the cat and therefore should not be part of their practices. After all, veterinarians went to school to protect cats, not couches!"

And declawing bans are better for cats in another important way: They can actually help decrease the number of cats relinquished to shelters, as demonstrated in Los Angeles, which banned the practice in 2009. The city conducted an audit of cat-intake numbers before and after the ban, and the findings were astounding.

"When the five years before the ban numbers were compared to the five years after the ban numbers, it became apparent that the declaw ban was keeping cats out of the pound, according to the head of Los Angeles Animal Services," says Dr. Conrad. "The number of cats relinquished to the shelters dropped by 43.3 percent after the ban went into effect, and adoption rates doubled."

That's undeniably "pawsitive" news for cats. Still, the practice continues for a variety of reasons. For one, cat owners may be uninformed about what the surgery involves. Secondly, declawing is a profitable procedure. "It became a common procedure that was offered with a spay/neuter, and veterinarians made easy and good money from it," Shepler points out. "This is why it is so hard to ban it here in America. Declawing is a billion-dollar business in America and, unfortunately, declawing vets and veterinary organization leaders won't put the welfare of cats over the welfare of their pocketbooks or their organization's pocketbooks."

Hopefully, it's now clear that declawing isn't a solution to keeping cats from scratching and that it causes irreversible pain and damage, which no kitty caregiver would want to inflict. But what if your cat is already declawed?

Myth: Declawed Cats Will Be Fine As Long As They're Kept Indoors

Most of us recognize that outdoor cats need their claws. After all, they need to scale trees to escape from predators and assess their surroundings. And they may need their claws as a defense if they're attacked by wildlife or another pet. But just because a feline is an indoor-only pet doesn't mean she doesn't need claws.

We've already outlined the myriad reasons that cats need claws to engage in instinctive behaviors and truly be cats. And it's clear that declawed cats can suffer from lifelong pain and even engage in unwanted actions, like biting and inappropriate elimination. However, cats may also need to defend themselves, even indoors, such as from another household pet.

And just because you intend to keep your cat indoors doesn't mean that your feline friend knows that or intends to honor your decision. Your cat may dash out the door as you're entering or exiting, or he may slip outside unnoticed through an open window. Suddenly your kitty is in a brand-new and possibly terrifying world and he's no longer equipped to protect himself.

Plus, indoor kitties still crave and deserve outdoor time. "Spending time outside provides tremendous environmental enrichment, but toe amputation disarms cats, preventing self-defense and escape," Dr. Downing points out. "Outdoor enclosures [such as catios, see page 204] solve this dilemma by allowing cats to spend time outside safely, protected from predators and neighborhood bully cats, but able to enjoy the richness of sights, smells, and sounds of the outdoors."

Healing a Lifetime of Pain

Felines are often in pain for the rest of their lives after toe amputation, and even doting owners might not realize it. "Declawed cats often suffer silently without anyone noticing the extreme pain they are in," Dr. Conrad says. "They might seem fine, but if they are sleeping a lot or hiding a lot, or are not confident or secure, these could be indications of pain and discomfort. Most [declawed] cats have, at bare minimum, intermittent pain, but more likely, some degree of chronic and phantom pain."

How can the owner of a declawed cat determine if their kitty is in such pain? Dr. Conrad suggests consulting with a pain-management specialist who's against declawing. Such an expert will be able to discern if a cat is a good candidate for declaw revision surgery, and they can also conduct pain trials to see how the animal responds. Because declawed cats' pain is often neuropathic in nature, the nerve-pain medication gabapentin is often prescribed. But a feline pain specialist may also suggest other medications, as well as physical therapy or laser therapy.

"It is easiest to assess cat patients' pain by taking them out of pain and noting their behavior changes," Dr. Conrad explains. "Often, once declawed cats are on proper pain management, they will begin to play and act more like a normal cat."

This has been the case with numerous declawed cats that registered veterinary technician Jeremy Ernst-Verhine has treated, especially two cats named Cooper and Maleficent. "In both Cooper and Maleficent's cases, they had a reputation for being antisocial, aggressive, and lazy cats," he recalls. "Once their pain was taken away—or at least better managed—they both became more friendly, less likely to lash out, more active, and more involved in their households. Behavior is the response to stimuli, and if you have a cat constantly bombarded with pain, that stimulus will result in undesirable behaviors. But if you take away that stimulus and replace it with better ones, the positive changes in behavior that follow are truly staggering."

In fact, a 2020 study published in *Fundamentals of Clinical Animal Behaviour* that looked at the role of pain and behavioral problems in cats and dogs concluded, "It is better for veterinarians to treat suspected pain first rather than consider its significance only when the animal does not respond to behavior therapy."

Alternatives to Amputation

Cat owners shouldn't resort to unnecessary surgery. Try one of these options instead.

1. Provide scratching opportunities. Give your kitty a variety of places and textures to scratch. Check out chapter 4 for guidance.

2. Trim those nails. With a little patience, nail trims can become a regular part of life for your cat and you won't have to worry about those little murder mitts snagging your sweater or your skin.

3. Put a cap on it. Nail caps can cover up the sharp tips of claws without interfering with normal cat behaviors, as long as your kitty tolerates them.

4. Use sticky tape or other deterrents to scratching furniture, as discussed in chapter 4.

5. Accept that scratching is a natural and normal behavior for a cat. Think of it this way: You may have carpet in your home and simply have to accept that someone is going to spill juice on it or track mud inside one day. Kids make messes. Heck, *adults* make messes. And so do cats. It's part of life.

Cat Tale: Taking Away Cooper's Pain

Jeremy Ernst-Verhine's senior tuxedo cat, Cooper, is healthy, playful, and truly living the best of his nine lives. Unfortunately, though, that hasn't always been the case.

Cooper was declawed as a kitten and lived the first few years of his life in his adoptive home, but when his owners had a baby, the cat began eliminating outside the litter box, so Cooper was returned to the veterinary clinic he was adopted from. He spent the next year in the clinic, which is when Ernst-Verhine met him.

"I felt bad for the little guy," he said. "[Cooper] was treated like a nuisance, shooed away anytime he approached an employee, kept in an exam room in the back of the building, given no toys or enrichment but just a single litter box and bowl kept full of dry food. I brought him toys, I sat with him, I bonded with him. When I left that clinic for another one, some of my former coworkers told me Cooper was wandering the halls looking for me, walking up to any

male client he heard and meowing at them, so I adopted him and brought him home."

Cooper had long had a reputation of being inactive, antisocial, and more than a little grumpy. But Ernst-Verhine, who'd recently started working at a clinic with Lynn, realized that maybe Cooper's behavioral issues were simply a side effect of lifelong pain from declawing. In addition to pain from the procedure, he also suffers from arthritis in his lower spine, knees, and hips, which is common in declawed cats.

To help, Ernst-Verhine began administering gabapentin to Cooper at a low level and slowly began to increase it. And the tuxedo cat responded very well.

"Once the dose got high enough, I noticed him becoming more active and social," Ernst-Verhine says. "As the dose got higher still, these effects became more and more pronounced and Cooper would demand affection and play. My biggest realization [about] the chronic pain he must have lived with his whole life came one day when I saw how he wanted to be a 'tree cat.' My wife and I built elevated walkways around parts of our house with stair-stepped shelves to allow access, as well as a mounted climbing pole. One day I walked into the hallway and noticed Cooper resting on the walkway there, observing everything from his elevated position and purring contentedly."

With his pain under control, his activity level up, and his transition to wet food, Cooper—who'd been obese for much of his life—also began to lose weight. And today, Ernst-Verhine says that Cooper lives "a much more comfortable life." Still, he wishes that Cooper hadn't had to suffer unnecessarily in his life.

"I do wonder what he would've been like had he been allowed to grow up with his claws," he says. "Somewhere in an alternate universe is a whole Cooper, running and climbing and being affectionate."

Kitty Care: How to Play
with a Declawed Cat

Play is an essential part of life for a happy, healthy cat. However, a lack of claws may deter a feline from engaging in play, not only because of chronic pain, but also because they simply struggle to partake in it.

"Amputating the last bone of each toe changes the biomechanics of the front feet," Dr. Downing explains. "Cats carry about 60 percent of their body weight on their front legs and feet, so altering the biomechanics in the feet changes how the entire body moves. This affects their balance, how they run, how they jump, and how they land when jumping down from elevated surfaces."

It's no surprise then that owners of declawed cats say that their pets have no interest in hunting, chasing, and pouncing. And can you blame them?

In addition to the pain they may be experiencing, they may also just not find joy in such activity. Just as the child who's good at sports enjoys playing sports, cats also want to pursue the things they're good at and enjoy. But without claws, they're not as capable of doing that, and they may choose to forgo opportunities for play. In such instances, it's clear that human intervention has truly altered the natural feline.

"Declawed cats can't catch slippery strings because they have no claws to get ahold of them," Dr. Conrad observes. "Declawed cats don't do as well with jumping games and are best on thick carpet when playing to avoid slipping and hurting themselves."

Of course, plenty of declawed cats continue to play, even if they do have difficulty balancing and grasping toys. But it's important to recognize that ambitious kitties that have learned to navigate their not-so-clawsome world are the exception, not the rule. "Some cats do better than others following toe amputation," Dr. Downing says. "It's important to understand that none of them are ever normal, though, as this procedure forever changes their anatomy."

(Continued on next page)

Still, there are ways to engage declawed kitties in play. You just need to take the proper steps and have the right equipment to make playtime accessible and satisfying.

1. Have your cat medically assessed. As we've said, a declawed cat that doesn't play may simply be in too much pain to do so. Get rid of the pain and the cat will be more likely to engage with you and with toys.

2. Make sure that there's proper footing. Play on a carpeted surface that's thick and soft, so your cat can get a firm grip and keep her balance more easily. Avoiding hard, slick surfaces will also encourage cats to jump and pounce.

3. Start slowly. Allow your cat to build confidence as he plays. Don't move the toy too quickly at first. Make it easy to catch the toy, and let your cat win often.

4. Shop with a declawed cat in mind. This was important enough to Lynn to actually design toys with them in mind. So look for toys they can more easily grasp, such as rings and loops, as well as toys that are soft to pounce on. Large kickers are also a good idea because they require the use of the back feet and declawed cats can hug the toy with their front legs. Also try small toys that can

easily be carried in the mouth, which can be great for cats to retrieve and play fetch with. Tunnels are another good option. However, don't just set the tunnel out and leave it—you need to engage with your cat in it. You can do this by running a stick alongside the outside of the tunnel and letting your cat bat at it from inside. You can do the same thing with a laser pointer, allowing your kitty to launch an attack on that elusive red dot from within his hiding space.

CHAPTER 6

What's for Dinner?
The Same Thing You
Had Yesterday

Your POV: My cat always has kibble in the bowl. What more could he want?	Kitty POV: Would you want to eat the same thing every day?

What if you could eat your favorite food every day? Maybe that's a deep-dish pizza, your mother's meat loaf, tacos from a local food truck, a heaping serving of pad thai, or a mouthwatering ice cream sundae. Or maybe your favorite food is a freshly opened can of tuna or the leftover milk in the cereal bowl. No judgment. "Purrhaps" you just have a lot in common with your cat.

But whatever food you crave the most, just consider treating yourself to it every day. Sure, maybe mom's meat loaf would start to lose some of its appeal now that a rare treat has become a daily occurrence, but it'd still be delicious. There's no doubt about that.

Now imagine eating it not just every day, but for every meal—breakfast, lunch, and dinner—for the foreseeable future. Sure, pizza for breakfast or ice cream for dinner could be a fun indulgence once in a while, but every day? Forever and ever? It probably wouldn't take long for your favorite food to lose its beloved status. You might even begin to dread mealtimes and have thoughts like, "Nachos and chocolate cake again? Can't I get some steamed broccoli here? Just for a change of pace?"

Clearly, eating the same thing every day—no matter how scrumptious it is—would be terribly boring. It would also take a toll on our health, since we require a variety of foods for proper nutrition. So it'd be absurd to expect us to eat the same thing for every meal, yet we typically expect our cats to eat the same thing for virtually their entire lives. Don't you think they'd like to change things up now and then, too?

Mix It Up Meow!

Cats crave a variety of foods, so if they're not getting an array of tastes and textures, they may try to find it themselves through hunting. In fact, this may explain why cats sometimes catch prey but don't always consume it.

You may have been told to feed your cat the same type of food every day, so you've stuck with the same brand and flavor of kibble or canned food for years. Perhaps one day, the store was out of your usual brand, though, so you tried a new one and saw firsthand the problem with changing your cat's food when Sir Meows-a-Lot became Sir Pukes-a-Lot. Obviously, you shouldn't have mixed things up.

But if you'd eaten only one food for your entire life and suddenly consumed something new, odds are you'd be feeling a bit sick, too. After all, your body has adjusted to taking in nutrients from only one specific source. If something new shows up, your gut bacteria would likely be as surprised as your taste buds.

However, feeding your cat a more varied diet is about more than just avoiding boredom, and it's a good idea to regularly change up your cat's food—unless, of course, your veterinarian has put your cat on a specific diet. "In addition to the boredom factor, there are other important reasons for feeding a variety of foods," writes veterinary journalist Ingrid King on her website, The Conscious Cat. She encourages people to "rotate different proteins, brands, and flavors" into their cats' diets.

For one, a variety of foods helps provide complete nutrition. While it's "almost impossible to find a truly deficient pet food in the United States today," according to veterinarian Dr. Patricia Lane, not all cat foods are created equal. In addition to different ingredients and amounts of those ingredients, there are also varying levels of quality among brands. Plus, a diverse diet helps cats maintain a healthy microbiome, the genetic material of all the microbes, which contribute to animals' immunologic and physiologic health.

"In terms of having evidence that feeding one food for life is best or whether feeding different foods is best, there isn't any," says veterinarian Dr. Joe Bartges, a professor of medicine and nutrition at the University of Georgia's Department of Small Animal Medicine and Surgery. "[But] I am a believer [in] food diversity—that is, feeding different types, brands, and consistency of foods. This prevents a pet from developing a specific food preference. And if there is a problem with a food, then that problem is minimized by feeding different brands, flavors, companies, and formulations."

Cats that chow down on a variety of proteins, textures, and flavors are less likely to get bored and turn their noses up at what you're serving.

A diverse diet can also prevent your cat from becoming finicky. Cats that chow down on a variety of proteins, textures, and flavors are less likely to get bored and turn their noses up at what you're serving.

In addition, just consider how you'd react if your doctor instructed you to eat the same thing forever or suggested that you feed your child the same food on a daily basis. "Imagine that your child has been born and you've taken him home from the hospital and things are going well," says veterinarian Dr. Andrea Tasi. "And your pediatrician said, 'Sure, Mrs. Jones, here's Dr. Tasi's Baby Chow. Do not feed this child anything else. Everything is complete and balanced in here.' Well, you would intuitively know that that [advice] was wrong. And yet we've bought it hook, line, and sinker from veterinarians and the pet food industry."

The Great Debate:
Wet Food versus Dry Food

One of the most commonly asked questions about the feline diet is whether wet food or dry food is better for cats. We can't definitively say that one is bad and the other is good. However, we do think it's important that our house panthers consumer wet food more often than dry food.

"I once heard a veterinarian say that dry food sucks the life out of cats," Dr. Lane reports. "That may not be entirely accurate, but the consensus in 2020 is that the majority of a cat's diet should be wet food."

Why should your cat mostly eat moist food as opposed to kibble?

For one, there's the issue of weight management. Studies have shown that the two greatest risk factors for feline obesity are an indoor-only lifestyle and the consumption of dry food. But consuming a diet primarily composed of wet food is beneficial because it's lower in calories than dry food. The average dry food for cats contains 3–4 calories per gram, while the average wet food contains 0.8–1.5 calories per gram.Secondly, the greater amount of water in wet food promotes urinary health and it can lower the risk of dehydration and constipation.

Thirdly, it's higher in protein.

So while the occasional kibble is fine, stick to cans most of the time. For example, you may feed your cat meals of wet food in a bowl or on a lick mat and then place dry food in puzzle feeders (more on this later in this chapter).

What to Feed Your Feline

Cats are obligate carnivores, or true carnivores, which means they must consume meat in order to survive and thrive. They can eat other foods, such as vegetables and grains, but they can't live off these alone. That's because felines don't have the physiological ability to digest vegetable matter and obtain nutrients from it. And they don't need to because the animals they consume have already done that for them. In other words, there's no such thing as a vegetarian cat.

"[Cats] can eat some grains and vegetables, but they must have meat," Dr. Lane says. "It doesn't have to be pure meat, or fresh, or raw, but some meat protein is required. Cats in the wild eat what they can catch. American cats dine primarily on birds and rodents, but they are not above scavenging through your garbage. The big cats can bring

down a pig or a gazelle, and the fishing cats of Sri Lanka have adapted to catch their own fish."

So what does this mean for your kitty's daily diet? It should be as similar to what a cat would eat in the wild as possible, but you don't need to introduce mice into your home to meet your cat's dietary needs. (Although, if you choose to go this route, there's no doubt your cat would enjoy it.)

Of course, with the variety of commercial cat foods available today, selecting one can be overwhelming. Luckily, pet food labels are just like the nutrition labels on human food, and the ingredients are listed in order of decreasing weight. So a cup of chicken will be listed before a cup of grain because it's heavier.

We know that protein is especially important to a feline diet, so take a look at what kind of protein a food contains. "All protein is not created equal," Dr. Lane says. "Eggs and shoe leather both contain a lot of protein. *By-product* is basically what is left over after the intended product has been made. In pet foods, it is usually excess organic materials remaining after processing human foods. It could be very good parts—think chicken livers or gizzards—or very scary parts—think chicken feet. And whole chicken means exactly that: the whole thing."

So we know protein is important for felines. After all, they're obligate carnivores. But that doesn't mean your kitty can flourish by eating just protein alone. Cats need to consume a healthy balance of proteins, fat, carbohydrates, vitamins, and minerals. While it's safe to say that cats naturally follow their own version of the Atkins diet (Catkins diet), there's still much debate about how many carbs cats truly need. Commercial dry cat foods contain more carbs that a cat would eat in the wild—and much more than a domestic cat would prefer to eat when given the choice, according to a 2017 study published in the *Journal of Veterinary Science*. And it's been hypothesized that a diet high in carbs contributes to medical conditions in felines, including obesity and diabetes.

However, if you feed your cat a rotating diet of foods, you don't need to get too hung up on reading all those ingredient labels, since your feline will be consuming so many different types of protein. "There is no right or wrong way to feed a rotation diet," King writes. "You can feed one food in the morning, and a different one at night. You can change foods weekly, or monthly. You can feed a variety of foods throughout the week. Some cats may experience mild [gastrointestinal] upset when changing foods, and the general recommendation is to introduce new foods slowly and gradually."

But keep in mind that different cats have different needs as they age. Kittens are growing rapidly, so they require different nutrients than an older or geriatric cat. And while the average feline needs to consume 25 to 35 calories per pound of body weight each day, less active cats need fewer calories. Plus, some cats may have medical conditions, like diabetes or renal disease, or they may be prone to developing urinary blockages, and require a specialized diet. Others may have food allergies. So it's important to talk to your veterinarian, but Dr. Lane advises to keep these three points in mind:

1. **Feed your cat multiple small wet meals per day. In the wild, cats don't consume large morning and evening meals. They eat numerous smaller ones (about 30–40 calories' worth/ one delicious mouse) throughout the day.**
2. **Offer a variety of foods. "Variety is the spice of life," Dr. Lane notes. "It keeps your cat open to many options and it prevents micro-deficiencies that might occur in [cats] eating the same food 24/7."**
3. **Give your cat some choice in the matter. "Your cat has a stronger opinion than any veterinarian," according to Dr. Lane. "To some cats, *no* really means no, and they will starve to death rather than eat that food. Do your homework, but listen to your cat."**

But *how* cats eat is just as important as what they eat.

Food for Thought:
Five Questions to Consider

Have a finicky feline? Here are a few other things to consider that may get your kitty eating and drinking.

Is the dish clean? It's not uncommon for cat owners to rarely wash their cat's dishes, but would you want to eat every meal off the same plate without washing it in between meals? Saliva and food remnants can quickly accumulate on a dish, allowing bacteria to flourish. Studies have found that pet food bowls are some of the most bacteria-laden surfaces in the home. So wash your cat's food and water dishes daily.

Is the dish comfortable? Some cats may experience what's known as "whisker stress" or "whisker fatigue," discomfort that occurs when a cat's whiskers touch the sides of the bowl when eating. While the jury is still out on whether this happens, you can offer your cat food in various types of dishes to see which one she prefers.

Is there competition? Cats are solitary hunters that kill small prey that they don't share with others—with the exception of mothers with kittens. So felines in multi-cat homes can experience stress if they're forced to share bowls or eat near one another. Even if your two kitties are the best of friends, and they love to snuggle and groom one another, feed them separately to prevent aggression or conflict over food resources.

Is the food located near the water? Cats in the wild may not drink from a water source near where they've just consumed their kill, since dead prey could contaminate the water. That's why many feline experts suggest that owners place their cats' food and water dishes in separate locations.

Is the food the right temperature? Cats typically eat their prey at "blood temperature," meaning it's warm. Cold (like that leftover canned food you stored in the fridge and dumped in the bowl) signals rigor mortis, which could indicate that the food is rotten and shouldn't be consumed. Hot food is simply unnatural and may even be uncomfortable for a cat to eat.

How to Feed Your Feline

Most indoor cats are fed once or twice a day in the same location. Or they may simply free-feed, their owners refilling their dish each time they notice that the kibble is getting low. Essentially, we dictate not only what our cats will eat, but also where and when. So the time and energy a cat must expend to eat is almost nonexistent. (Unless, of course, your cat is in the habit of expending a great deal of energy to wake you up for his 4 a.m. feeding, but more on that later.)

The truth is that this couldn't be more drastically different from how cats eat in the wild. And when cats are permitted to choose their own eating schedule, they tend to eat the way their ancestors and unowned cousins would. They hunt, which cats are designed to do, they eat a variety of prey, and they consume small meals roughly eight to sixteen times a day.

"In the wild, they spend six to eight hours a day hunting, performing 100–150 attacks each day, successful only about 10 percent of the time," Dr. Lane notes. "And even though cats have a preferred prey, nature provides a lot of variety: fat mice and skinny mice, birds full of seeds and birds full of worms. [They eat] ten meals today and one tomorrow. So felines are active, persistent, and designed to eat multiple small wet meals each day. Doesn't sound much like cat life in our houses, does it?"

However, there are ways we can provide our felines with a more natural feeding experience, which can improve both their health and their happiness. The unnatural way most indoor cats eat has been linked to boredom, which can lead to both under- and overeating. And this type of feeding can also contribute to both physical and behavioral problems.

But there's an easy fix—and you don't have to release your cat into the wild to hunt her own dinner, nor do you need to keep live

prey on hand for feedings. (Again, that's an option, but just think of the mess!) Instead, simply create opportunities for your cat to "hunt" and forage with puzzle feeders. In other words, let your cat play with his food!

Puzzle feeders, or food toys, are devices that cats must manipulate in various ways to obtain food, and certified cat behavior consultant Beth Adelman says they should be an essential tool for every cat owner. "That's just nonnegotiable," she maintains. "You gotta have food toys."

There's no shortage of puzzle feeders available for purchase, but you can also make your own with household objects like paper bags, paper towel rolls, and jars and plastic containers. We're big fans of simply using paper plates or paper lunch bags to hide kibble or treats. Simply place 10 to 20 pieces of food, which is roughly 40 calories (and about what a cat consumes in a meal) on each plate or in each bag and hide them throughout the home. This lets your cat discover meals throughout the day, just as they would in the wild.

The bags can be especially fun for felines because they can rip them open to claim their prize.

In addition to providing felines with both mental and physical enrichment by encouraging natural feeding behaviors, puzzle feeders can also help cats slow down as they eat, preventing gorging and vomiting.

And while lots of puzzle feeders and food toys are designed for kibble, plenty are available for kitties on wet food–only diets as well. For example, you can use paper plates to deposit small amounts of food on, or you can purchase a lick mat.

You can also vary the time, place, and delivery method for your cat's food. Perhaps you hide food toys throughout the home that your kitty can seek out when she's actually hungry. Maybe you provide morning wet food on a lick mat and create hunting opportunities in the evening while you're watching television by tossing pieces of dry food down the hallway. Or you may learn your cat's preferred times to eat and adapt her feeding schedule to fit those.

Kitty Care: Foods to Share

Cats are curious by nature, and if your cats are anything like ours, they're often curious about what's on your plate and what's in your bowl. So if you're in the mood to share, here are some kitty-safe foods that felines can sample. Just keep in mind that these are meant to be the occasional indulgence, not a meal replacement, and that not every food on this list will agree with every cat's stomach.

Laura's cat Fiver's "purrsonal" favorite human food? Corn on the cob. He can't get enough of it! Lynn's cat Roo's favorite food is pizza!

- Bread
- Dairy items, like milk, creamer, plain yogurt, or butter. (Licking the butter wrapper or the yogurt lid can be an exciting treat!)
- Eggs (cooked)
- Fruit, including bananas, blueberries, cantaloupe, and pumpkin
- Grains, like corn, couscous, oats, and rice
- Meat, such as chicken, salmon, turkey, and liver that's cooked and unprocessed
- Vegetables, including broccoli, carrots, green beans, peas, and spinach

"There has to be some middle ground there where cats get to make some choices," Adelman says. "I've had clients say things to me like, 'Well, [my cat is] hungry at night,' and it's like, 'Well, if he's hungry at night every single day, why don't you feed him at night?' Why does he have to be on your schedule? I think cats really suffer when they have no choices and when they have no control."

As your cat becomes more adept at solving food puzzles, make or pick up more complicated ones. Plus, many puzzles come with various levels, so you can adjust the difficulty for your pet.

However, think of puzzle feeders as toys, items to use occasionally to enrich your cat's life. Maybe you love crossword puzzles, for example, and enjoy doing one during your daily lunch break or while you have an afternoon snack, but do you want to be forced to solve riddles every time you eat a meal? Surely not. So continue to feed your cat in her dish, but mix things up by using puzzle feeders on occasion.

> "Cats really suffer when they have no choices and when they have no control."

Kitties Need Their Greens, Too

Your diet isn't complete without greens, and the same goes for your cat. Yes, kitties are carnivorous, but they still require occasional roughage. Plant matter has been found in the scat of numerous feline species, indicating that there may be an adaptive significance to plant consumption in cats' evolution. And a 2019 survey of 1,000 cat owners found that 71 percent of them had observed their pets gobbling greens.

Why do cats do this? That's still a bit of a mystery. "If anyone truly knows the answer to that, they are not sharing it with the rest of us," Dr. Lane notes.

You may have heard that cats chow down on grass to induce vomiting, but that's not necessarily the case. Ninety-one percent of respondents in that survey said their cats didn't appear ill before consuming grass, and only about 25 percent of those felines vomited after eating greens. So researchers theorize that vomiting is simply an occasional by-product of eating grass—not the objective. (However, it's worth noting that scientists didn't look into whether consuming grass helps expel hairballs.)

The researchers who conducted this study hypothesize that cats, much like chimpanzees and other animals, nosh on grass to help them remove intestinal parasites by increasing muscle activity in the digestive tract. While your average indoor housecat likely doesn't have such parasites these days, the grass-munching behavior remains.

Dr. Lane offers another possibility, though. "Mouthfeel is very important to cats," she says. "Maybe grass-eating reminds them of the juicy little mousey intestines that they chewed on as a kitten. Maybe that is why they also eat string and ribbons and sewing thread. Maybe they need grass to keep them from eating much more harmful things."

You may have provided your feline friend with grass before, but removed the greenery from your home after cleaning up some green regurgitation. But don't let the occasional mess deter you from doing right by your kitty. Odds are, your cat was so excited to engage in the instinctive behavior of greenery gobbling that she overindulged. "Cats that don't have regular access to grass tend to eat too much too fast when they do find it," Dr. Lane explains. "Small amounts frequently go down better."

Plus, providing grass that kitty can happily munch means she's much less likely to turn her attention—and her teeth—to your beloved houseplants.

Grasses and Safe Indoor Plants for Cats

- Catnip
- Valerian
- Alfalfa
- Wheatgrass
- Barley grass
- Oat grass
- Mint
- Rye
- Cat thyme
- Licorice root
- Lemongrass

Hydration Is "Impurrtant"

You know you're supposed to consume at least eight cups of water per day. Perhaps you carry a water bottle with you everywhere or even track your H_2O consumption with an app. While your cat doesn't need to drink nearly as much as you do (cats need 3½–4½ ounces of water for each five pounds of body weight), hydration is still essential for felines. And many cats aren't consuming as much as they need, which can lead to health issues.

While your cat may have constant access to water, the lifestyle of *felis interius* can actually contribute to dehydration. Why? Oftentimes, it's because water dishes aren't kept clean or refreshed daily, as they should be. But a cat's diet can also contribute to dehydration.

Felines evolved to get water from their food, so a cat that consumes dry kibble alone may not get enough H_2O. Switching to, or adding, wet food to your cat's diet can go a long way toward helping your pet stay hydrated. But there are also steps you can take to entice your cat to drink up.

Introduce running water into your home by getting a fountain or turning on the occasional faucet. Cats may prefer to drink from a moving water source—and they often have a great time playing in it as well.

You can try moving your cat's water bowl to a new location in the home, preferably one away from her food, as well as adding additional water bowls. You may also want to experiment with different types of dishes, such as shallow ones that can be more comfortable to drink from if your cat experiences whisker fatigue. In addition, you can make your kitty's water more appetizing by freezing low-sodium broths or tuna juice in an ice cube tray and dropping the occasional cube into the water. But again, make sure to regularly clean that dish!

Not sure if your cat is getting enough water? You don't need to break out the measuring cups and eye dropper to ensure that your 10-pound cat is actually drinking those seven to nine ounces of water a day. Instead, simply pay attention to your pet and figure out his usual behavior.

"Cat parents should be aware of how much water consumption is normal for their cat, just as they watch for normal amounts of urination, which equates to water loss," Dr. Lane points out. "Changes in either are red flags. It is also important to know what normal, moist, pink mucous membranes look like. Sticky, tacky membranes indicate dehydration. So take a look at your cat's gums. Are they shiny and moist? She's hydrated! Are they dry and dull? It's time to hydrate."

"Similarly, healthy, well-hydrated skin springs right back into place when it is pinched up. Dehydrated skin holds that pinch shape for one to two seconds. Old cats sometimes have old lady skin that is slow to return to place. Just know what is normal for your cat."

Kitty Care: How to Avoid a Hairy Situation

Hairballs, which, despite their name, aren't usually round, are a part of life for cats and their caregivers. Because cats tend to be fastidious groomers, they naturally ingest loose hairs. Most of this hair passes through cats' digestive tracts, but some of it collects in the stomach and is eventually disgorged.

But while hairballs are normal, hacking up more than a few a year isn't. "There is a misconception that frequent furballs are normal for cats," says Jodi Ziskin, a certified pet-nutrition consultant. "I've had many clients hire me over the years because they were looking for a more natural diet plan for their cat, not realizing that this issue would be resolved."

If your cat has frequent hairballs, consult your veterinarian to ensure that your own feline fur baby is healthy. Your vet may suggest changing your cat's diet to help with the issue. Hypoallergenic diets, high-fiber diets, and hairball-control gels and treats can help reduce hairballs.

Brushing your cat often can also help remedy the problem. "Any hair you can toss in the garbage is hair that won't be swallowed and redeposited on your floor in the form of a hairball," observes veterinarian Dr. Jennifer Coates.

CHAPTER 7

From Idle Paws to Active Paws

Your POV: I've tried playing with my cat, but he doesn't want to play.	Kitty POV: I love to play. You're just not playing the way I like.

When you were a child, how often did you turn to a parent, friend, or guardian and complain, "I'm bored"? If you're a parent, how many times do you hear that sentence on a daily basis? And how many syllables has your progeny managed to add to the last word?

Even those of us who aren't parents, or who haven't been children ourselves for quite some time, have certainly had the thought. We may have been stuck in a staff meeting, counting down the minutes until the bell rang at school, or trying to find something to occupy our time during the sixth long month of quarantine, but the feeling was the same.

Our cats understand this feeling of boredom, restlessness, and despair even better than we do, though, because, for them, it's been their entire lives. They're captives in our homes, and any change that occurs within their prison—whether it's a new piece of furniture or a novel scent wafting from the kitchen—occurs because of us.

But while we've all been bored before, we've never been *indoor-cat bored*. This level of boredom is endless and repetitive, and it's exacerbated by the fact that cats have little to no agency in their own lives. As much as they may want or need something, they likely can't get it. And this boredom goes much deeper than simply a lack of things to do.

The lack of physical activity and mental stimulation that indoor cats must contend with day after day and year after year affects them more deeply than we could possibly understand. It takes a mental toll, often resulting in anxiety and depression. And it has physical effects as well, which can manifest as serious health ailments, such as skin conditions and gastrointestinal disorders. Veterinarian and certified feline behaviorist Dr. Rolan Tripp frequently attributes these health issues to what he calls exercise frustration. In other words, cats are unable to engage in necessary activities, which creates increasingly high levels of stress.

Lack of physical activity and stimulation takes a mental toll on cats, often resulting in anxiety and depression.

The psychological stress causing medical symptoms with exercise frustration can cause urinary problems, gastroenteritis, loose stools, and vomiting, according to Dr. Tripp, as well as a skin disorder known as idiopathic ulcerative dermatitis (IUD). This skin condition is associated with a crusted, self-induced ulcer that often appears on felines' necks and backs, where scratching and grooming occur. Researchers once considered this to be a disease of unknown origin. But a 2018 study found that cats suffering from it could recover in just two weeks simply by modifying the animals' environments to make them more enriching. This incredible finding even resulted in the researchers' suggestion that the condition itself be renamed.

"These results suggest that feline IUD is a behavioral disorder indicative of poor welfare and that it requires management by behavior specialists, proposing environmental modifications," reads the paper, which was published in *Frontiers in Veterinary Science*. "We hence propose to rename this affliction to 'behavioral ulcerative dermatitis.'"

The physical manifestations of stress that cats suffer from shouldn't surprise us. After all, we've experienced the side effects of stress ourselves. When our bodies are flooded with cortisol and adrenaline, our heart rate increases, our muscles tighten, and our blood pressure increases. We can become moody or depressed, and we may experience headaches, upset stomach, muscle pains, insomnia, and other physical symptoms.

Clearly, our mental well-being is directly related to our physical health, and it's no different for felines. "The biggest killer of animals is not a powerful virus or poisonings; it's behavior," Dr. Tripp says. "Exercise frustration is one of the primary stressors of felines, and that mental distress is causing the two most common reasons for cats to go to the vet—intestinal and dermatologic."

Providing opportunities for cats to be active and exercise doesn't only heal many common ailments, but it also has myriad other health benefits. "Physical exercise brought on by exploring and playing has multiple benefits that go beyond energy expenditure and burning calories, and contribute to overall well-being," says feline behaviorist Anne-Claire Gagnon. "It increases mental stimulation, improves muscle mass, and therefore enhances your cat's metabolism, it enhances mobility and blood flow, and, when playing in your company, it naturally reinforces her bond with you."

Five Reasons to Play with Your Cat

We've touched on a few reasons you should grab a wand toy and engage your cat in play, but here's a full list that'll highlight the power of play.

- To improve your cat's quality of life
- To deepen your bond with your cat
- To keep your cat mentally and physically healthy
- To help your cat vent excess energy
- To alleviate problem behaviors like aggressive biting or bullying

Playtime: Rules of the Game for a Healthy, Happy Cat

Create a hunt. Playtime is all about the hunt for your feline friends, so if you want to create an exciting playtime experience, you have to engage with them in a way that allows them to tap into their natural hunting instincts. Think about how your kitty reacts when he sees something like a fly buzzing through the room or a squirrel moving outside the window. He crouches down low, his pupils grow larger, his butt begins to wiggle, and he may even chirp or vocalize as he gears up for the pounce. So when you're playing with your cat, look for these behaviors to ensure that your cat is truly tapping into the hunter within.

Also, consider how a cat would hunt in the wild. What catches his attention? Often, it's the bird fluttering and landing nearby, or it's the chipmunk with its back turned as it rustles in the leaves. Once something has your cat's attention, he watches it, stalks it, and performs a series of impressive calculations about how far to jump and how much propulsion he'll need.

So play with your cat so he can tap into these skills and behaviors. Don't wave a wand toy in front of your cat's face and expect him to move into full-on attack mode. Have you ever seen prey jump in front of a predator and do a little dance? Of course not. Instead, move the toy as prey would. Flutter it through the air and have it land for a few seconds before taking flight again. Have it move across the floor and dart around a corner, disappear behind the couch, or dive beneath a blanket. In other words, allow your cat to hunt the toy just as he'd hunt a bird or an insect that found its way indoors. This allows your pet to truly be a cat.

"When your cat is indoors, your cat doesn't have the ability to express all of her natural behaviors," says Kitten Lady Hannah Shaw. "If you think about a cat in the wild, they're very attuned to everything that's going on. Anything that moves they're going to notice and be curious about. And if it seems like it's a prey item, they're going to pounce on it and have this full range of physical and emotional experiences attached to that hunting process. But a cat who's indoors is really missing out on both the physical and emotional parts of hunting. So since we are controlling everything about the environment in our home and nothing changes in our homes unless we change it, we have to create these hunting simulations for our cats."

Mix it up. Cats don't hunt only one type of prey. They stalk squirrels, pounce on rats, and leap for moths, so you need to provide your kitty with a variety of "prey" to hunt indoors as well. And, no, you don't need to set a family of rodents free in your house. You simply need to have several types of toys available to keep your cat interested.

These include passive toys that cats can bat around and play with on their own, such as balls, springs, catnip mice, electronic items to chase, and more. But to keep these toys interesting for your kitty, you can't just leave them lying around all the time—then the toys become just another unchanging element of the home. Instead, regularly rotate your cat's toys. Put a few away and reintroduce some other toys that your cat hasn't seen in a while. This helps them maintain their novelty because there's always something new in the environment. You can also locate several toy baskets or boxes throughout your home and change up what you store in each one. This gives your cat opportunities for discovery. Plus, she may even enjoy just digging out the toy that's caught her eye.

Active toys are ones that your cat enjoys with you, such as a wand toy. These are especially exciting because they're something your feline friend gets to do *with* you, his favorite human. So make this type of play a regular part of your day. For example, make playtime

part of your morning routine while you sip your coffee, or engage your kitty in some leaps and swats for a good 15 minutes before bed, so you'll both be tuckered out. Lynn stores wand toys in the closet as a reminder to play with her cats morning and evening when she changes clothes.

When playtime is over, put these toys away as well. This ensures that the interactive toy is fresh and exciting each time it comes out. Plus, it's safer for your kitty not to have access to toys with long strings that could be ingested.

As a kitty caregiver, you've no doubt seen your cat turn virtually anything into a toy—your shoelaces, a wine cork, a bottle cap. Use this as "inspurration" and invent new toys and games for your kitty as well.

"Sometimes the best toy is taking a piece of computer paper and crinkling it into a ball and throwing it," Shaw says. "Sometimes I turn just a piece of dry food into a toy and throw it down the hallway, and the cats are excited because it's this little thing running down the hall that they can eat. I call it 'Treat Toss,' and Treat Toss is a favorite game in my house because it's not like you're just handing a treat to your cat or putting a treat on the floor. When you throw it, they chase it because they're hunters. It's really exciting when they see something small moving down the hallway. So they chase after it, and, even better, it's edible."

You can also create a fun challenge and tap into your kitty's love to forage by filling a box with some brown packing paper. Then toss treats inside the box, so she can rummage around and find a snack.

Make it rewarding. If you struggled with and lost every round of your favorite game—whether it's basketball, Scrabble, Fortnite, or Cards against Humanity—you'd probably lose interest pretty fast. And the same goes for cats, which is why it's so important for felines to "win" or catch their "prey" when they play.

So when you and your kitty play, make the "hunt" challenging, but not impossible. And adjust how you play based on your cat's needs or skill level.

Provide cats with toys they can sink their teeth and claws into—so their win can be truly satisfying.

For example, kittens may not be coordinated enough to catch a quickly moving toy just yet, or, if a cat has mobility issues or is geriatric, it wouldn't be fair to dangle a toy several feet in the air.

"We want our cats to feel like, 'Wow, I'm a good hunter. I had a challenge, but I caught it,'" Shaw said. "Remember that you're the one who's creating the feeling that there is prey in the home, so you want to give them a little bit of a challenge, but not so much of a challenge that they think they're a bad hunter. Let them catch it, let them bunny-kick it, let them bite it, let them do all the things they're going to do with their prey."

This is why it's so important to provide cats with toys they can sink their teeth and claws into—so their win can be truly satisfying. "We need to allow cats to truly catch toys, which is why I'm not a big fan of laser pointers, for instance," Shaw says. "Cats and kittens need to feel like they've truly caught their prey." So instead of engaging in a round of tug-of-war, let your cat run off with his catch.

At the end of the play session, you can even give your cat a favorite treat. After all, if Fluffy were truly a wild outdoor cat, she'd be enjoying the spoils of her catch. "Give them some kind of food reward, because that would be the natural next step—that they would eat something after catching their prey," Shaw concludes.

Do This, Not That: Mistakes People Make When Playing with Cats

DON'T wave a wand toy in a cat's face. That's not what prey does.

DO move the end of the wand the way prey would move. Flutter it into the air or skim it quickly across the floor and around the corner.

DON'T constantly feverishly wave the wand around the room.

DO let the toy land and sit still, giving your cat time to attack.

DON'T play tug-of-war with a wand toy.

DO let the cat catch the toy, enjoy his spoils, and then play another round.

DON'T prevent the cat from ever catching the toy.

DO let him win and sink those claws and teeth into his catch.

DON'T give up too easily. If your cat doesn't respond to one toy or game, try another!

DO allow plenty of time for cats to watch and stalk their prey.

Games for Indoor Kitties

Just as your parents or teachers provided you with rainy-day activities as a kid when you couldn't go outside to play, indoor cats require the same kind of distractions. So, in addition to daily playtime with your cat, it's also important to occasionally give your cat a little something new to try to explore. Here are a few games to play with your kitty.

- **Footsie:** We've all seen kitty paws appear under a closed or partially closed door. Use a wand or other toy to give your cat something to attack.
- **Knock-Off:** Cats love to test gravity, so deliberately place nonbreakable items on shelves and tables where your cat likes to hang out.
- **Bed Bugs:** Grab a wand toy, ruler, or stick and run it beneath the sheets, so kitty can pounce.

- **Fetch:** Lots of cats love to fetch. (In fact, all three of Laura's do. The dog? Not so much.) Throw a small toy that your cat can easily fit in his mouth, such as a soft ball, and let him retrieve it.
- **Bubble Pop:** Bubbles aren't just for kids. Cats also enjoy chasing and popping bubbles. Be sure to pick up cat-safe bubbles—you can even get your paws on catnip-scented varieties.
- **Treat Toss:** Simply toss a treat down the hall or across the room, and let your cat give chase and chow down.
- **Peekaboo:** Duck behind the bed or another piece of furniture and poke your head out every few seconds, and watch your cat creep up on you. You can also capture your kitty's attention by grabbing a pillow or cushion and peering around it for a game of peekaboo.
- **Hide-and-Seek:** Hide scented toys around your home and let kitty follow the trail to capture her prey.

Clicker Training

A wonderful way to keep your cat active and engaged indoors is with clicker training, a training method that rewards desirable behaviors. Not only does clicker training keep cats active and engaged, but it's also an exciting way to interact with your feline friend.

"One of the benefits I've noticed when we train is that Tarantino is less inclined to act out for attention," said Niki Malek. She began looking into clicker training as a way to "deter Tarantino from behaviors like climbing up the windows, attacking the plants, and 4 a.m. parkour." She learned that instead of focusing on the behaviors she didn't want Tarantino to engage in, she should direct his energy toward other behaviors, such as going to a target station or lying down.

"Now, [Tarantino] sleeps better at night, especially when we have a training session close to bedtime," Malek said. "There's also this inherent satisfaction of working on a new behavior and seeing it finally click. Maybe that's more for me, than Tarantino, but it's just a lot of fun to witness."

All you need to get started with this type of training is a clicker (you can also use a click-top pen, a clicker phone app, or a sound of your own) and a reward. The reward is often a yummy treat, but you can also provide positive reinforcement with attention and praise or playtime with a favorite toy.

The sound of the clicker doesn't mean anything to the cat at first, so you need to charge the clicker, or associate the clicking sound with a reward. Begin by simply making the clicking sound and immediately following it with the reinforcer or reward.

Next, select the behavior you'd like to encourage. This could be a variety of things, but it's a good idea to start with a behavior that comes naturally to your kitty, such as sitting, looking at you, or sniffing an object like the end of a stick. As soon as your cat performs the desired behavior, click and provide the reinforcer.

When your cat is consistently doing the behavior you want, add a verbal and/or physical cue. For example, you may say "sit" or "high five," or you may simply hold your palm toward your cat to indicate that you're asking for a high five. So let's say you've been working on teaching your cat to sit. You've already taught the behavior by using a click and a reward. Now, as you hold a treat or target stick above your cat's head, you'll notice your cat moving into a sitting position. At this time, say, "Sit," and as soon as he's sat, click and give the reward. Once you've established this new pattern, start giving the verbal or physical cue sooner so that your cat performs it at your command.

Now that your cat has learned one behavior, you can start adding others. Do a few minutes of training each day to keep your cat stimulated and to get a little one-on-one time with each other.

Here are a few more tips to help you get off on the right paw:

- Keep training sessions short.
- Only click once to indicate a desired behavior.
- If your cat performs the wrong behavior, don't click. But don't punish her, either. Cats don't learn through negative reinforcement.
- Never attempt to move your cat into the desired position, such as by grabbing his paw to make him give you a high five.

And, most importantly, be patient. "Be patient with your kitty and the progress that is—or seemingly isn't—being made," Malek says. "Be observant of your kitty's behaviors while training and flexible to adjust for optimal learning. And, last but not least, start with a simple behavior to build confidence. Everything builds from a solid foundation."

Myth: Some Cats Just Don't Play

All cats hunt, so all cats play. And just because your kitty has all her meals regularly provided doesn't mean she doesn't still have the instinct to stalk and pounce throughout the day.

If your cat doesn't seem to play, she may simply not have the outlets to engage in these behaviors as she'd like to—she may not have the kinds of toys she wants to chase and attack. She may even have resorted to creating her own toys, swatting at your feet as you pass by or batting a scrap of paper across the floor.

Cats that don't play may also be sick or in pain, so it's important to talk to a veterinarian to get to the bottom of the issue. For example, a senior cat may have arthritis, making it painful to climb and pounce. And declawed cats may have difficulty keeping their footing or grasping toys, which deters them from playing.

Felines may also be depressed or simply indifferent to toys because after years of inadequate or inappropriate toys—or a lack of owner involvement in playtime—they simply no longer try to to play.

Cat Tale: Kitten at Heart

When Dana Widmer rescued a 14-year-old cat named George from Animal Control, the senior kitty was labeled "semi-feral." But when she brought George home, she quickly realized that he wasn't feral at all—he was simply fearfully responding to his environment.

Now in his forever home, George was a bit more social, but he was still having trouble adjusting.

"George was very nervous [about] all the changes and became very vocal, especially in the night," Widmer recalls. "He was quite the agile boy at his age and would jump each night up into the

ceiling area of my basement room and cry because he had trouble getting down. Once I blocked off the area and added some [pheromone] diffusers and soft music, it was time to work on making him feel comfortable."

George was warming up to Widmer and enjoyed her petting and other shows of affection, but despite all his energy, he wasn't interested in play or toys.

"He acted like he didn't know what to do with them," Widmer says. "I would try wand toys, mice, and balls, and every night I would throw around little toys to try to get some interest. He just stared at them."

Then, one day, Widmer played some bird videos on her iPad, and the chirps and fluttering wings immediately captured George's attention. "I quickly realized he loved it and was very engaged," Widmer notes. "This boy was a hunter at heart."

Once she understood that George was indeed interested in play (aka hunting), Widmer recommitted herself to bringing out the kitten in her senior cat.

"Several days passed, and I found a soft mouse toy with a long tail," she notes. "For days, I moved it around, trying to get him to play. Still nothing. Until one night I threw it to him and suddenly he kicked it back to me. This turned into a game of back-and-forth with the mouse toy—I threw it, and he kicked it back. He grabbed it, kicked it with his back feet, and kicked it back to me. It's as if he was learning to play for the very first time."

This game and that mouse remain among George's favorites to this day, but he's since expanded into other types of playtime and engaged in more natural cat behaviors.

"He looks forward to our play every day," Widmer observes. "He is more of an interactive player and wants me to join in. He now enjoys cardboard scratchers and catnip toys, too, which he will play with independently. George is definitely now living the kittenhood that I believe he never had."

CHAPTER 8

Stereotypes, Stigmas, and "Meowntal" Health

Your POV: My cat's physical needs are met.	Kitty POV: There's much more involved in my emotional health than you realize.

It's estimated that one in four adults has a diagnosable mental illness, according to the National Institute of Mental Health. And during 2020 those numbers skyrocketed, when the COVID-19 pandemic forced many of us into our homes for months on end, and threatened our lives and livelihoods, and those of our loved ones. A survey in May 2020 found that more than a third of US adults had symptoms of clinical anxiety or depression.

However, while a survey by the American Foundation for Suicide Prevention found that 90 percent of Americans believe that physical and mental health are equally important, they don't receive equal treatment. This isn't surprising, given the host of stigmas associated with mental illness. In recent years, though, Americans have begun to discuss mental health and mental illness more openly, and now it's not uncommon to see these issues featured in television plotlines or hear them mentioned on podcasts. And one upside to the pandemic is that 16 percent of people who said they were uncomfortable talking about their own mental health issues prior to stay-at-home orders now report that they're comfortable doing so.

Clearly, attitudes and perceptions about mental health are changing, and we hope this is good news for cats, too, because we're not the only ones who suffer in silence. Felines are also subject to depression, anxiety, and other mental health issues.

"Cats have the same neural chemicals that cause depression in us," says certified animal behavior consultant Steve Dale. "Do [cats] get depressed by reading the newspaper or watching TV? No, the same things don't depress them. But they can get depressed, and one thing that seems clear is that indoor cats don't get to make choices and aren't able to do what they want to do. Why wouldn't that cause depression?"

Oftentimes, felines' declining mental health goes undiagnosed and untreated. Some attentive kitty caregivers may immediately notice changes in their cats' behavior and take action. However, many other cat owners may have simply accepted some of these behaviors as normal or even relinquished their pets to a shelter because of them.

Symptoms of a mentally struggling cat typically manifest as behavioral problems and can include any of the following:

- Aggression, predation, and inappropriate play
- Fearfulness and skittishness
- Elimination outside the litter box
- Urinary complications, such as straining to eliminate
- Excessive grooming, sometimes to the point of causing self-induced wounds and hair loss
- Lack of grooming (unkempt hair or coat)
- Overeating or a loss of appetite
- Lethargy
- Oral or dietary indiscretions, such as eating or chewing nonfood items, like plastics

As we've discussed in previous chapters, indoor cats' mental and emotional well-being is closely associated with their environment, so it's no surprise that a life of captivity with little to no change isn't only draining, but also damaging.

"I think that the greatest disconnect between clients and their kitties right now is in the perception of emotional well-being," asserts board-certified veterinary behaviorist Lisa Radosta. "As we can all see now that we have been in our homes more than is typical since March 2020 when COVID hit us hard, living within the four walls of our homes can be maddening. Cats don't have any hope of leaving and they don't often even get to go outside. This can lead to lots of behavior problems."

The indoor-only life certainly takes its toll, both on us and on our cats, but there's another facet of feline indoor life that's also worth exploring: the emotional drain of living in such close proximity to people.

To help us better understand this, consider the relationships you've had over your lifetime, whether they're familial, platonic, or romantic. You no doubt know someone who leaves you feeling drained after every interaction. They could be pessimistic, hyper-critical, or simply self-involved. They may complain incessantly, have a negative take on everything, or feel compelled to unload on you emotionally so that you feel you're carrying their burdens. Regardless, they leave you feeling depleted, which is why psychiatrist Dr. Judith Orloff refers to such people as "emotional vampires."

Veterinarian Dr. Andrea Tasi thinks we can have a similar effect on the felines we share our homes, our lives, and—even if it's unintentional—our feelings with. "There's a burden of living with people," she points out. "[People can] ask too much of the bond between a cat and themselves. People will say, 'This [cat] is my soul mate. She's the only one who understands me. She is my family.' And part of me goes, 'Yep, I get that.' But part of me says, 'This is a cat. This is not a person.'

"And projecting that kind of energetic responsibility or burden onto a cat, an animal who is exquisitely emotionally sensitive, I think is very, very hard on these animals. I do believe that our companion animals are inordinately trying to help us and give of themselves in ways that they will become ill if too much is asked of them. That translates to a hyper-attachment to the cat. I think that is exhausting to the cat on an emotional level."

Steven Ray Morris, cohost of the Purrrcast, a podcast for cat people, echoes this sentiment. "I think a lot of times people adopt pets out of a need for something," he notes. "But animals aren't here to do our bidding. You have to remember that this is a living creature that you have a relationship with and you're going to get from it what you give, so that's what you have to be willing to do. I think my relationship with my cat, Penny Lane, has always been at its best when we're sort of actively communicating our needs. I mean, one of us is meowing and the other is . . . well, I guess I'm often meowing, too . . . But the point is that we both have to listen to each other and pay attention and give as much as we take."

Our feline friends do pay attention to us, and they can and do pick up on our emotions.

Because the truth is that our feline friends do pay attention to us and they can and do pick up on our emotions. Oakland University researchers found that cats can read human facial expressions and they learn this ability over time, so the more time they spend with a human, the more adept they can become at reading our emotional cues.

Of course, many of us already know this. After all, we've seen how our own cats respond to us emotionally.

When we're feeling down, we may crawl under the covers and be immediately joined by our cat. One of Laura's cats, Fiver, purrs and rubs against her almost frantically when she's upset, and it's certainly a comfort. The cuddles of a purring feline can be soothing, and we may assume that our cat is comforting us. Science itself may not agree just yet, but there's undeniably a connection between cats and their owners. It may simply be that, over time, cats have learned that our sad emotional states come along with plenty of pets and attention, which makes them more likely to seek us out when we're exhibiting signs of sadness.

But there's also plenty of anecdotal evidence that our feline friends know when we're upset or in pain and that they respond to our feelings with concern and affection, even if they can't experience and process those emotions the same way we do.

"If you speak to people who are chronically ill, they will explain that their pet will lie across the part of their body that needs healing," Dr. Tasi says. "Well, that's the animal trying to give healing energy . . . I don't know whether it's even a conscious thought. It's not like the cat goes, 'Oh, I know Mom's got ovarian cancer.' It's just a thing that they do."

Suffice it to say that we might be an emotional drain on our indoor cats, just as some people are to us. And that makes the plight of *felis interius* even more complicated. But Dr. Tasi is quick to point out that the burden of living with people is actually a two-sided one for cats. On the one hand, we may sometimes ask too much of our cats on an emotional level, but on the other, cats may actually feel unfulfilled by their lack of relationship with us. Sometimes we may even subject indoor cats to both experiences by needing a lot from them emotionally one day, but leaving them lonely and despondent when we're not home, often for days at a time.

"The other side of that two-sided burden [of living with people] is being ignored," Dr. Tasi says. "We think, 'You know, I can be gone for a week if I just leave food and it's no big deal.' A friend of my sister's has a cat, and he travels all the time. So that cat just sits in the apartment all by herself. What is that cat's mental, emotional health? Probably pretty bored, but not very put upon. She probably doesn't feel that she has to keep him happy the way I think a lot of animals feel that they have to give up themselves in some way." (It should go without saying, but never leave your cat alone for days.)

The emotional and mental health of *felis interius* becomes even more complex when we consider how often the cats we bring into our homes—homes they may spend their entire lives in—come from outdoor-living situations. The move inside is both mentally and physically jarring and requires adjustment. Just consider how your own mental health might be affected if you suddenly found yourself living outdoors with none of the modern technology and conveniences—no electricity, climate control, or smartphone—that you've become accustomed to.

"Cat emotional health has been greatly affected by [where some of] our cats come from, the fact that we are sourcing our cats from feral, stray, nonsocialized populations," Dr. Tasi says. "I think it's causing a real problem that we're self-selecting for animals who are less social, more anxious, bringing in that feral sort of thing. I think early-age spaying and neutering, especially in males, is also driving this. If we're neutering these males before they ever get a whiff of testosterone . . . Well, testosterone makes you brave. It makes you stupid, but it makes you brave. And so I just see a lot more cats who are really fearful."

It makes sense that indoor cats would be more fearful than their outdoor counterparts. After all, they spend their entire lives within four walls, where life remains essentially the same day after day. In the outdoors, cats are exposed to a plethora of stimuli in the form of sights, scents, and sounds. They lounge in the sun, dig in the dirt, sample the grass, listen for the scurrying of rodents, watch birds take flight, follow intriguing scents, and more.

Indoor cats, of course, experience their own stimuli, but they're often of the unnatural variety: the roar of the vacuum, the noise of the dishwasher, the scents of cooking food and chemical cleaning agents, the taste of the often highly processed food we feed them. But these stimuli quickly become familiar and typically follow a routine, so *felis interius* often responds to something new or different in his environment with fear.

And all that fear? It leads to chronic stress and anxiety that can manifest as physical health issues. So it's no wonder that indoor felines are prone to becoming overly sensitive scaredy cats.

Do Felines Really Have "Cattitude"?

Just as stigmas are associated with mental illness, stigmas and negative stereotypes are associated with cats. And these are important to highlight because they affect how we view and treat the cats in our homes, as well as the feline species as a whole.

When PetSmart Charities asked survey participants to describe cats, a majority of people said that cats are intelligent, loving, cuddly, and attractive. However, they also selected a lot of negative words, including moody, stubborn, aloof, and grouchy. Fewer than half of respondents said cats were friendly, protective, or loyal—words they readily associated with dogs.

We asked numerous people—both feline advocates and those we'll call "feline detractors"—what other negative adjectives they've heard associated with cats. The list was long: spiteful, antisocial, vicious, stupid, mean, picky, finicky, dangerous, vindictive, and even evil.

You probably know someone who'd agree with these descriptions, someone who claims they've known or owned a cat themselves that was obviously demonic and out to get them. But, surely, we can all agree that these are a lot of emotions to ascribe to an animal that, although intelligent, is, to our knowledge, incapable of actually experiencing them.

Take our tendency to say cats are spiteful, for example. "Spite takes so much complexity of thought," says feline behaviorist Beth Adelman. "It's about holding in that anger, saving it, figuring out what's going to annoy the other person, and then waiting until a moment where you can perform that. Cats don't have that complexity of mind."

The commonly held belief that cats are aloof and indifferent to their caregivers also doesn't hold up, and there's even scientific research to support this. "People care about whether cats really do understand and pay attention to their owners," Dr. Jennifer Vonk, a

psychologist at Oakland University, told the BBC. "Our work shows that they may not be as indifferent as people accuse them of being."

Other feline stigmas that really claw at "expurrts" like Adelman include calling cats "divas" and referring to them as "antisocial."

"We call them divas because they have preferences," she explains. "Am I a diva because I like chocolate ice cream better than strawberry? That's what I say about pickiness. We all have preferences, so why shouldn't they? And antisocial? One of my cats, when I adopted him, was labeled as 'indifferent to human handling.' And so now, when he jumps up on the top of his cat tree and rolls over on his back and begs me to touch him and I'm kissing him on his tummy and he's purring, we always make the joke about how 'indifferent' [he is]. I think probably 99 percent of cats in the shelter are terrified, and you're not yourself when you're terrified. So we have no idea who they really are, right?"

Yet we continue to make assumptions and assign labels to cats that can actually harm them. Partly, it has to do with popular culture and how felines are presented, and often demonized, within it.

"There's a lot of comics and graphics out there that like to make fun of cats because those of us who have cats like to tell stories about cats," says Becky Robinson, president and founder of Alley Cat Allies. "We anthropomorphize and turn them into little humans and make up stories that are not really real. Like, if we're gone for a few days, we say cats are mad at us. Or when people say they think their cat knows something is right or wrong [or that] they're plotting against us. But cats aren't thinking that way. It's not like they take this etiquette class. They're not trying to be a certain way or not.

"One of the things that comes up is that cats have attitude, which means they have a bad attitude. There was even a calendar called 'Bad Cats' and it was, again, a joke, but it adds to the whole stereotype. I do think that words matter—my grandmother told me that. And [these words] conjure up an image. We are not helping cats when we use those words because, while we don't *want* to paint cats in a bad light, we inadvertently do."

The negative labels we assign to cats aren't assigned to them simply by self-professed "cat haters," though. We're also guilty of anthropomorphizing, for example, and creating entire narratives about our own cats. After all, we've certainly been known to joke about how a cat woke us up at 3 a.m. as "revenge" because earlier we interrupted his afternoon nap with the vacuum cleaner.

Sometimes, these negative stereotypes are popularized and reinforced even by the people who care for them. For example, when Laura took a kitten that I was bottle-feeding to a veterinarian, both the vet and the staff joked about what a handful this kitten would surely become. "Bottle babies are spoiled brats," more than one person said offhandedly. It's a common stereotype that Hannah Shaw says breaks her heart.

"It really upsets me when people say that bottle babies are poorly behaved because that's not been my experience whatsoever," she says. "The stereotype makes me sad because if there is a bottle baby who's 'poorly behaved,' that may mean they didn't have everything that they really needed as a baby."

And the words we use to describe cats don't only affect the ones we keep as pets, but also free-roaming cats that live outdoors and aren't suited for indoor-cat life. For example, calling a cat "feral" could quite literally cost that cat her life. The negative connotation of a word like *feral* often results in these cats being killed, and it's why animal-welfare organizations like Best Friends Animal Society insist on calling these felines "community cats" instead. As Robinson's grandmother said, words matter.

Myth: Cats Are Low-Maintenance Pets

There's a tendency to think of felines as low-maintenance animals, especially when compared with dogs, but nothing could be further from the truth. There's the widely held belief that as long as there's food and water left out and a relatively clean litter box nearby that cats have everything they need to thrive. Again, this isn't true.

Dogs, however, need more space, require trips outside, plus frequent attention, toys, and regular vet visits. But cats need these things, too.

And when we perpetuate the myth that cats are low-maintenance, we're doing harm to our feline friends because they don't receive the care, resources, and attention they need and deserve.

So the next time you hear someone say that they're getting a cat because they don't have time, space, or money for a dog, remind them that caring for a cat is just as involved, and requires just as much investment and commitment, as caring for a canine.

A Cultural "Purrspective"

It's also imperative that we consider how our culture's and our society's view of cats impacts felines. Yes, this is a book about cats, but it's also a book about our relationships to and with cats—and not just the personal relationship with our beloved pets, but also our relationship with the feline population as a whole. Because this big-picture, cultural view of cats impacts how we both perceive and treat the species. So let's kick things off by sinking our claws into a stereotype we're all familiar with: the crazy cat lady.

There's long been a connection made between the feline and the feminine. And it actually goes much deeper than just the notion of the "crazy cat lady," which, by the way, is a stereotype that nearly 50 percent of Americans buy into, according to that PetSmart Charities survey.

For centuries, cats have been associated with women and, of course, witchcraft. There was a time that it didn't take much for a woman to be accused of witchcraft, and sometimes simply owning a cat was "proof" enough to make such an allegation. Cats, after all, weren't just pets—they were often thought to be gifts from the devil. And people believed that a cat might not only be a witch's familiar, but also a shape-shifting witch herself.

Black cats, of course, which easily blend into the shadows until we spot their glowing eyes, took the brunt of the "bad luck" backlash. These superstitions still persist today, which is why some shelters and rescues won't adopt out black cats near Halloween out of concern that the animals may be abused, an antiquated belief that can do more harm than good.

We may think that modern society has moved beyond such negative associations of women and cats, but if we scratch below the surface we find that's hardly the case. References to cats occur not only in the occult, but also in art, culture, and even politics, and they're frequently coded as female, with negative connotations.

You can see this in the stigma of the "crazy cat lady," the spinster with dozens of cats and no male human companion. But you can also see it in the overtly patriarchal concept of the "sex kitten" or the casting of an older women in the predatory role of a "cougar." We even hear it more subtly when someone—almost always a woman—is said to be "catty" or involved in a "catfight." These negative links between women and cats are deeply ingrained in our language.

It's not uncommon to hear all cats referred to with feminine pronouns and all dogs with masculine ones. In fact, columnist Barry Thompson wrote an entire essay on the gendered phenomenon for *Esquire* after yet another person assumed that his male tuxedo cat was female.

There are numerous theories as to why we assign gender to animal species. Some hypothesize that it's because dogs exhibit more stereotypically male behavior, being outgoing and simple to read, whereas cats are associated with stereotypical female behavior, being sly and mysterious.

"There is something to the inherent femininity that cats seem to have carried with them," Morris says. "People see cats as mysterious and almost duplicitous, like we don't know their true intentions. But, hey, maybe cats are like, 'You don't deserve to know my intentions, bro. You're just an acquaintance, so you get to stay at paw's length.' And I respect that about cats. I *want* there to be a mutual respect. Men liking cats is a thing. This is not a totally alien concept."

"Somehow society associated cats with women, and it's like men have a harder time being interested in cats because it's seen as weak or something," says the Purrrcast cohost Sara Iyer. "But cats are so cool and ferocious, whether they're male or female. It's like there's this binary of 'male or female' or 'cat or dog' that's just incorrect. Every animal is different."

Unfortunately, though, American culture hasn't caught up with Iyer's outlook. A 2020 Colorado State University study found that women were less likely to swipe right on men who pose with cats in their dating profiles. The men in the study were viewed as more open and agreeable, but also less masculine.

The study's authors say their findings are the result of cultural stereotypes about cat and dog owners. "It is important to note that these findings were influenced by whether the female viewer

self-identified as a 'dog' or 'cat' person, suggesting that American culture has distinguished 'cat men' as less masculine, perhaps creating a cultural preference for 'dog men' among most heterosexual women in the studied age group," the study reads. "Women prefer men with 'good genes,' often defined as more masculine traits. Clearly, the presence of a cat diminishes that perception."

There's a lot to theorize about here—and a lot to unpack—around the feline and the feminine, but that's another book entirely. For now, let's just say there's no denying that felines' association with the feminine hasn't always worked in cats' favor.

Putting aside some of the most egregious crimes humans have committed against felines—such as their mass slaughter in the 1400s due to the belief that cats carried the Black Death (they didn't), but also the crusade against witches and their kitty companions—let's instead return to the dichotomy we've created between cats and dogs and see how this has contributed to our lack of understanding of cats.

Dogs are called "man's best friend," but it wouldn't be far off base to say they've also earned themselves the title of "researchers' best friend," at least when compared with cats. Much behavioral and social cognition research has been focused solely on canines.

Conduct a search of published papers on cats and dogs and you'll find hundreds of thousands more on canines. And yet, aside from dogs, no animal besides the cat is as prevalent in our homes, nor as beloved. "The scientific output doesn't match the popularity of cats," cognitive ethologist Ádám Miklósi told *Science* magazine in 2019. "We know more about how wolves think."

Why is this? Because cultural attitudes and biases have crept into research, according to Dr. Elinor Karlsson at the Broad Institute and the University of Massachusetts.

"The research has lagged behind in cats," she told the *New York Times*. "I think they're taken less seriously than dogs, probably [because of] societal biases. Non–cat people tend to laugh at the idea of studying behavioral genetics in cats, and the animal training world complains that people tend to dismiss cats as untrainable." (We cat lovers know this couldn't be further from the truth, though. Sure, our cats are trained to come running when they hear the treat bag rattle, but those of us who have clicker-trained our cats are well aware that cats can learn all sorts of tricks, from sitting and spinning to rolling over and giving high fives.)

The problem with this lack of feline research, especially from a behavioral perspective, is that humans tend to protect and prioritize what we understand. On the other hand, it's all too easy to avoid, dislike, or even outright fear what we don't. Certainly, the mysteriousness of cats

Cats are more like dogs—and a lot more like us— than we think.

appeals to many of us, and we value and even respect felines' complexities. But if we look at how cats are viewed from a big-picture cultural perspective, the dichotomy is clear: Dogs are man's best friend. Cats are . . . well, not.

So feline behavioral research is important not only because it informs us and makes us better able to care for cats, but it also helps dispel the very stereotypes that can harm felines and our relationships with them. Because when we actually conduct the behavioral and social cognition research, what we find is that cats are more like dogs—and a lot more like us—than we think. "There's a very widespread belief that cats are stupid and selfish," says Péter Pongrácz, an ethologist at Hungary's Eötvös Loránd University. "The new results are pushing back on that."

What have scientists learned about cats that many people would find surprising? (Not you, though. You've likely known this all along.) Here are just some of the highlights researchers have discovered when they turn their focus to felines:

- Cats opt for human social interaction over food, meaning they're just as loving as their canine counterparts.
- Cats, just like dogs and even toddlers, know that when humans point at an object, we're instructing them to look at it. Most animals, including even our closest biological living relative, the chimpanzee, fail this experiment.
- Cats know their names and will respond to them—even when an unfamiliar voice is calling them. Of course, whether they choose to acknowledge your call is another question entirely.
- Cats look to their owners for cues and shape their behavior to human emotions. For example, when a new object, such as a fan with crackling streamers, is placed in a room with a cat and her owner, most cats (79 percent) look to their human for reassurance. If the human responds positively— for example, saying, "What a nice fan" in a soothing voice— the cat understands that the object doesn't need to be feared and will usually approach it.
- Cats are more likely to slow-blink, the feline equivalent of a smile, when someone slow-blinks at them first.
- Cats respond to human emotional cues, often rubbing against their owner when the owner is sad or upset.

We hope it's evident now that felines are more complex, more capable, and more like *us* than you once thought. Because the truth is that how we perceive cats and how we talk about them influences how we treat them, which affects not only the physical health of *felis interius* but also the animals' mental and emotional well-being.

CHAPTER 9

"Furiends" and Enemies

Your POV: The cats will learn to get along or they'll keep to themselves and be fine.	**Kitty POV:** Sometimes I'm scared in my own home.

Do you remember what it was like to walk the halls of your middle school? During your first few days, you didn't only have to learn your way around and adjust to a new schedule, but you also had to avoid potential conflicts and attempt to make friends, the whole time wondering if you're wearing the right shoes, if anyone has noticed the zit on your chin, and if that guy in the cafeteria thinks you're cute or is planning to steal your lunch money. Maybe you made friends easily and quickly assimilated into the new social dynamics of junior high. (Well done. Let us know what that was like.)

But perhaps you had a hard time. Maybe the halls felt unsafe—whether from the shove of a bully or the judgmental glares of your peers—and you kept your head down, hurrying to class, hoping you'd reach your destination unscathed. Perhaps you struggled to find where you belonged and ate lunch alone or purposely hid out in the bathroom or library to avoid other people. Maybe this time in your life was an absolute nightmare, where threats both physical and emotional loomed around every corner.

Now imagine that you can never escape this situation. School isn't just five days a week, but instead 24/7. The bully threatening you may be lurking around every corner, lying in wait to pounce. Any time you enter a room, you might suffer a confidence-shattering insult or physical attack. Your fear and anxiety are relentless, and that takes a toll on every aspect of your life. It affects your appetite, your sleep, and your blood pressure. Virtually every waking thought is one of risk assessment. Your world gets smaller and smaller as you retreat to whatever place you feel most safe. Or maybe, instead of withdrawing, you lash out, pick fights, and become an aggressor yourself. Regardless, one thing is certain: You're not only unhappy, but you're also unwell.

While this is certainly a nightmare scenario for many American teenagers, unfortunately, it's also the heartbreaking reality for many indoor cats. There are approximately 96 million cats living in US households, and the number of multi-cat households is on the rise. This is definitely good news for some cats. After all, there are millions of cats in shelters and plenty of felines live better lives because of kitty companionship. But, as many cat owners are well aware, not all cats in multi-cat homes are living their best life. Lots of them are trapped in the feline equivalent of junior high.

Cats are often thought to be solitary creatures, but the truth is that the social environment is actually very important to them. In the wild, felines hunt on their own, but they often live in groups of up to 20 cats. Felines' social behavior is influenced by how they were socialized as kittens, and those that were raised in groups tend to adapt to life in multi-cat households better than kittens that were raised by their mothers or humans alone.

"Cats are not unsocial," Dr. Lane says. "They just have to have the right environment. Cats live in social groups made up of related individuals and contact with total strangers is kept to a minimum. Socially bonded pairs are most often mother-kitten or siblings, and these cats will all rub or groom one another. This is a clear signal that they are socially bonded. In the wild, when there is plenty of food and space, related female cats will actually share dens and nurse one another's kittens. Strange cats *can* form social groups, but it is relatively rare. But cats that are not part of a socially bonded group can coexist peacefully if the environment is right. They just have to be able to control the situation and have an outlet for their energy."

So in the wild, cats have two things that *felius interius* doesn't: space and choices. A solitary tabby in the outdoors can opt to distance herself from other cats, establish her own territory, and live an independent life. Or she can decide if she wants the company of other cats and attempt to join a colony. This is typically a slow process. She may be chased away when she first approaches the group, but if she keeps returning, she'll very likely be accepted into the colony over time.

> "Cats are not unsocial. They just have to have the right environment."

This gradual acceptance process actually mirrors the way a new feline can be accepted into a multi-cat home. With that in mind, let's take a look at some of the common problems multi-cat households face, how kitty caregivers can help overcome these challenges, and proper cat-introduction techniques that can help avoid inter-kitty conflict from the get-go.

It's All about Resources

When cats feel threatened, physically or emotionally, they may react in a variety of ways. They may become aggressive, they may withdraw, they may exhibit anxious behaviors, such as overgrooming, and they may even become physically ill. Cat behavior expert John Bradshaw has said that one of the most surprising elements of his feline research has been his realization of how susceptible cats are to stress and how much they can be negatively affected by it without their owners even being aware of it.

In addition to injuries inflicted upon one another, felines in multi-cat homes may also experience chronic stress. And experiencing the body's flight-or-fight response for long periods takes a toll on the mind and the body.

"[More cats are mysteriously getting] dermatitis and cystitis [inflammation of the bladder] and it's becoming abundantly clear that these medical problems are made worse by psychological stress," Bradshaw told *National Geographic*. "[For instance], inflammation of the bladder wall is linked to stress hormones in the blood. [Plus,] other than routine visits, the most common reason cats are taken to vets is because of a wound sustained in a fight with another cat."

What exactly leads to conflict among felines in multi-cat homes? Oftentimes, it's competition for resources. This may surprise you. After all, your cats each receive the same number of meals per day, they all have access to the same beds and scratching posts, and they snack on the same number of treats every afternoon. But just because you allocate the resources evenly or just because they're available to every cat in the house doesn't necessarily mean that your cats feel that distribution is fair or that they're actually consuming or using those resources in the same way.

Twenty-four percent of indoor cats don't have their own food bowls, instead being forced to compete for kibble from the same dish. And more than half of indoor cats share a single litter box. These situations lead to resource guarding, defensive behavior, and even outright aggression.

But it's not just food, water, and litter that cats compete for; it's also sunny spots, perches, toys, beds, and attention from *you*. While it may not seem to you like there's any threat to these resources—after all, your cat likely hasn't posted himself as a sentry in front of the litter box to prevent the others from using it—another cat may still perceive such a threat. She may not have as much control over her environment as she'd like or have the status or rank among the other cats that would help her feel safe. This creates a contradiction between what your cat needs and desires and what she's actually able to accomplish or possess. And that's hard.

Picture yourself in middle school again, lonely and lost. You wander into the cafeteria on the first day of school, lunch in hand, looking for a place to sit and eat. You don't see any of your friends, there's not an empty table to be found, and the girl who's been tormenting you since fourth grade whispers something to her friends, and they all glance your way and start to laugh. Your stomach turns, your face heats up, and you're suddenly not so hungry. All you wanted was a friendly face—or, at the very least, a seat where you could go unnoticed while you scarfed down a sandwich—and now you just want to flee. You want to escape the situation immediately and find a way to feel safe again.

With that scenario in mind, imagine how a frightened, anxious cat feels every day when she wanders over to the food bowl, stomach growling, only to be stared down by another cat as she eats. Or even chased off, pounced on, or bitten. Now she's not only uneasy and hungry, but she's also injured. That's no way to live. Don't force your cat to eat in a middle school cafeteria.

So one of the first places to start to avoid or resolve inter-cat conflict is to ensure that there are plenty of resources to go around, starting with individual bowls. Just imagine if your parent or guardian had placed three servings of food on a large plate and expected you, your sister, and your brother to all eat from that one plate. Sure, there's enough for everyone, but not everyone is going to consume the same amount. Someone is going to eat someone else's share, whether it's accidental or intentional, whether they steal it when someone isn't looking or they shove you out of the way.

It may even be necessary to separate cats at mealtimes to ensure that everyone has time to eat without the fear of another cat finishing first and rushing to snag the other's leftovers. Owners can also invest in electronic feeders or cat doors that open only for one particular cat, based on their microchip. This way, cats can eat on their own time without interruptions or any thieving mouths. Simply ensuring that felines in a multi-cat home have individual access to one of their most important resources—food—can go a long way toward preventing conflict among them.

The same goes for another extremely important resource: the litter box. Multiple litter boxes are essential for multiple cats. And, as we discussed in chapter 3, cats need not only choices in type of box and type of litter, but also in litter box location. When placing litter boxes in a multi-cat home, owners should also consider how a box's location might affect the cat approaching or exiting the box. For example, if the favored litter box is located in a small room with only one access point, this can cause stress and lead to conflict because it's easy for a cat to become trapped inside, in an attempt to avoid a cat that may be lying in wait to pounce.

Meet Your New Best Friend/Lifelong Nemesis

Some conflict may always exist in a multi-cat home. That's unavoidable, regardless of species. If you grew up with siblings, you're well aware of this. One moment, you and your brother may be getting along great, the next, you're pulling his hair and he's wrestling you to the floor, and you vow to never speak to him again, and he tells you that you're not his real sibling anyway (your parents found you, lying unwanted in an alley), and you tell him that you're the one who broke his favorite toy, and he retaliates by hiding *your* favorite toy, and you start to yell at him, and he says he wishes that for once you'd honor your vow never to speak to him again, and next thing

you know you're both fuming in separate rooms because Mom couldn't take it anymore, but we digress—back to cats.

So the occasional cat fight just comes with the territory of having to share space and resources with someone else. Squabbles happen. Someone will inevitably snatch a catnip mouse from the other or swat at the other's tail just because they're bored, and things will escalate and you'll find yourself saying the cat parent equivalent of "Don't make me turn this car around!"

These types of conflicts are especially likely when a new feline is introduced into the home. Again, those of us with siblings may relate if we can recall what it was like to go from being the only child, your parents' pride and joy, to the being big sister or big brother. Suddenly, there's someone else in the home who's not only taking up your space and grabbing your toys, but also monopolizing your parents' attention. It's not uncommon to hear stories of older siblings who resented the new baby or even went so far as to hurt them or try to get them into trouble so that their parents would see what a mistake it was to bring this new being into the home.

Cats feel the same way. The arrival of another cat isn't only scary (*Who is this guy? Why does he smell so weird? Will he like me? What if he hates me? What if he steals my food? What if the humans love him more than they love me?*), it's also a very real physical threat (*He's bigger/faster/stronger/more aggressive than I am. He could hurt me. I need to run/hide/hurt him before he has the chance to hurt me.*) Does this all sound a lot like middle school or is that just us?

So before a cat owner brings another animal into the house, especially another feline, it's essential to consider how the existing cat will feel about that change. Unfortunately, we can't sit down and have a heart-to-heart with Fluffy about how, when Mommy and Daddy love cats very, very much, sometimes that means a kitten is about to appear in the house. But what we can do is honestly ask ourselves how a new feline addition might change the home's dynamic and how that might affect Fluffy's health and well-being.

The truth is that, if he had the opportunity and ability to tell us how he feels about the idea of a new cat moving in, Fluffy would very likely say, "No, thank you." However, while Fluffy may be resistant to the new cat at first, eventually he'll most likely become very closely bonded with Fluffy #2. Unfortunately, it's impossible to predict how cats will react or how their behaviors and relationships will change over time. What's the best we can do? Carefully consider the decision to expand your feline family and take the proper steps to ensure that the introduction goes as smoothly as possible.

So when it comes to introducing a new cat into the home, take it slow. Don't drop a new kitten or a new cat of any age next to your current cat and leave them to work it out. If you do, there's likely to be swatting, hissing, and growling, and someone might get hurt. (What if a stranger suddenly appeared in your living room? Would you throw an arm around her and invite her to stay for dinner, sleep in your bed, and live the rest of your lives together? Uh, no.) Instead, start by setting up your new cat with her own safe, private area and food, water, bed, toys, scratcher, and litter box. "The cats should not be asked to share critical resources until they have shown themselves to be comfortable living together," Dr. Lane says.

Let this cat get comfortable in this new space, and let your other cat get used to the idea that there's someone else on the other side of the door. "The cats can then hear one another, smell one another, even play under the door with one another," Dr. Lane points out. "Many people find that it is very easy to replace a bedroom door with a screen door so the cats can see one another."

You can also gently rub the cats with a soft cloth, focusing on areas with scent glands like the whiskers and paws, and place these scented items beside the other cats' beds or dishes. This can help them get used to the other cat's smell. But *don't* rub that cloth on one cat and then rub it on the other. Don't force one cat's scent onto another cat. Again, it's all about providing choices and letting a cat take that step when he's ready. You can also swap the cats' scratchers or bedding to help them get used to the other's scent.

And you can feed them or give them treats on each side of the door, or even with the door cracked open a bit, so they can begin to have a positive experience (tuna!) they can associate with the new kid in the house. "It's desensitization and counter-conditioning," Adelman explains. "There are no shortcuts for a slow and careful introduction. There are just no shortcuts. Even when you put cats on two sides of the gate, you can't control how those cats are experiencing that." And that's why it's so important to give them time to adjust.

As the cats get more comfortable with one another, you can open the door a bit more and let them sniff one another. You can provide them with supervised time together and attempt to distract them and engage them with play. Praise them and reward them for positive interactions and recognize when it's time to give the cats a break from one another.

Even the most slow and careful of introductions likely won't go off without a hitch, however. Hisses will be exchanged, some swats, pounces, and bites as well. If the situation escalates and one or both of the cats becomes aggressive, avoid the temptation to get involved or try to separate the cats yourself—this could lead to injury. Instead, make a loud, sharp noise. Slam a door, bang a pan, clap your hands, or stomp on the floor. Then, try to distract the cats with a favorite toy. With time and conditioning, though, hopefully your cats will learn to coexist, even if they never snuggle together, groom one another, or exchange friendship bracelets.

In general, Dr. Lane says that cats that initiate interactions with people tend to be more open to interactions with other cats. However, even if your current cats are the best of friends, who share meals and toys and would totally be each other's bridesmaids, it doesn't necessarily mean that they're going to like another cat. Or, if your cat's companion passes away, don't assume that he wants or needs someone else to keep him company.

"A cat who has another cat friend doesn't mean that they're going to like every cat," Adelman says. "I get this all the time. You know, 'Sam died last week, and so we're going to bring in a new cat.' And just because Fluffy loved Sam doesn't mean he's going to love anybody else. I'm actually very bonded to my husband [Craig]. We're a bonded pair. What if he died tomorrow and then two weeks after that, another guy knocked at the door and said, 'Hi, I'm your new husband.' The fact that I bonded to Craig doesn't mean necessarily that I would even want this other guy in the house, right?"

Even if you have two cats that coexist peacefully, that doesn't necessarily mean that both of your cats actually like each other—or always will. Relationships change over time. (Do you still hang out with your childhood best friend? Did you actually marry your high school sweetheart?) And when the social dynamics of the home change because one of those cats passes away, owners may be surprised by how the remaining cat's behavior changes.

"When you have a pair of cats, you'll have one who's more interactive and one who's less interactive," Adelman observes. "If the more interactive one goes first, the less interactive one suddenly becomes [cuddlier]. And you think it's because 'Suddenly he loves me more,' but really no, he was hanging back [before]. He was hanging back because the more interactive cat was kind of monopolizing that resource, which is you. So if you find your cat suddenly becomes more interactive when the other cat dies, they don't want [another cat]. They want time alone with you."

Of course, sometimes it's a good idea to bring multiple cats into a home together. Kittens, for example, are full of energy and tend to thrive when they have a companion to wrestle with and snuggle up next to. Many shelters and rescues even require kittens to be adopted together, or they allow single-kitten adoptions only if there's already a cat or dog in the home.

However, if you have an older cat that's content in your home, bringing a kitten into the mix likely isn't going to be a welcome addition. "Do not ever [get a kitten] to be friends with your older cat because, first of all, that kitten is for you," Adelman says. "It's not for your older cat. It's just like if your eighty-year-old grandmother is lonely, the answer is not to get her a two-year-old to live with."

Can All Cats Learn to Get Along?

Can all people learn to get along? As much as we wish the answer were yes, sometimes that's just not the case. "Social bonding is a fragile thing, and only the cats know why it works or doesn't work," Dr. Lane says.

"There is not a road map or a one-size-fits-all solution to cat relationships," says Deb Barnes, author of *Makin' Biscuits: Weird Cat Habits and the Even Weirder Habits of the Humans Who Love Them* and founder of Rainbow Bridge Remembrance Day, an internationally recognized day on August 28 that's devoted to the celebration of the pets we've loved and lost. "Just like a human, each cat has a distinct personality and range of tolerance for companionship. It's okay if not all your cats are best friends but with patience, perseverance, and trial and error, at the very least you can usually get them to coexist."

Talk to your vet and consult with a certified feline behaviorist to exhaust all other options, but it's up to you to ultimately make the difficult decision in the best interests of all the felines in your care. And if you decide to keep all the cats in the household, ensure that each of them has their own resources. Don't force them to share food, water, litter boxes, scratchers, or toys.

"You [can] do a careful and considered introduction and two cats [may still] just really hate each other no matter what," Adelman points out. "[In that case,] the best solution is to rehome one of the cats because it's just terrible for two beings to be forced to live in a concise, confined space when they hate each other and one is afraid of the other. That's just no way to live. Those cats are better off not living together in the same house . . . like when people get divorced. You know, sometimes you're just better off apart."

Kathy Copeland understands this all too well. She and her husband bonded with their foster cat Anna and wanted to make her a permanent family member. They tried countless times to integrate her into the home with their other cats. But Anna, who was loving and affectionate to her human caregivers, had no such love for her new siblings. The other cats' presence made her feel threatened, and she'd lash out, and Copeland worried about both Anna's safety and the safety of her other cats. Ultimately, she made the tough decision to let Copeland's mother adopt Anna instead. Now Anna is the only cat in the house and gets all the attention and affection she desires. Anna has never been happier.

Don't assume that your cat wants or needs another cat to keep him company.

Myth: Cats Aren't Social Animals

There's a tendency to compare cats and dogs, but they're very different animals with different social structures. Cats have their own ways to show affection, and although they may be independent creatures, they still crave attention and can suffer from separation anxiety.

This Guy Smells Funny . . .

As we've said again and again, scent is important to cats. They sniff items—and people and other animals—to learn more about them. They avoid a stinky litter box. They scratch to leave their scents behind and mark their territory. They use scent to create a familiar social environment or "scent profile" in a home. They may even attempt to cover leftover food, feces, or other smelly stuff they come across.

So it should come as no surprise that the scent of another cat is incredibly important. After all, the same can be said for us. When we're seated next to someone with body odor on an airplane, we lean away and it negatively affects our entire travel experience. And scent is intimately linked to sexual attraction and even important in the success or failure of a relationship. It's not so different for our feline friends.

Laura experienced this firsthand when her cat, Sirius Black, came home from a vet checkup only to be hissed at and attacked by her other cat, Fiver. Sirius Black and Fiver grew up together, snuggle together, play together, and even groom each other. If they could exchange friendship collars, they would. But, suddenly, Fiver was acting like Siri was an unknown invader, and he wanted nothing to do with him.

This may be difficult for us to understand. Shouldn't these cats recognize each other? But while scent is important to us, it's a much bigger deal to cats. So think of it this way: A young child may not recognize a parent or guardian who's dressed up as Santa Claus, but when the costume comes off, suddenly that loved one is familiar again. In the case of felines, the other cat has come home in what's essentially a "scent costume," making one cat essentially unrecognizable.

It took several days and an entire reintroduction process, but eventually Fiver accepted Siri again and they were back to snuggles and grooming sessions. Still, this occurs every time one of them visits the vet—even if they go together. The culprit? The unfamiliar smell that lingers on them after a trip to a new location where they're handled by several people, swabbed with alcohol, and they've picked up scents from other animals.

Scent may also be to blame for two cats that Dr. Lane previously treated. "I once worked with a couple of cats who had been a socially bonded pair for more than ten years," she recalls. "One of the cats suddenly started violently attacking its longtime friend, frequently drawing blood. This went on for weeks, while I wasted a lot of time and money trying to find out what was wrong with the cat who suddenly turned mean. When I finally discovered that the victim cat was diabetic, and treated him accordingly, all of the aggression disappeared."

Diabetic cats can develop sweet- or fruity-smelling breath, a sign of ketoacidosis, giving the animal an unfamiliar smell.

So what's a cat owner to do if their cats suddenly start acting strangely or aggressively after a visit to the vet or a trip outside? Separate the cats to give them time to get reacquainted, switch their beds or blankets so they can refamiliarize themselves with each other, allow them to groom themselves so their scent profiles return to normal. There's no set time you have to wait—it could be several days. That's why Lynn tells all of her clients to give the cats plenty of time to thoroughly groom themselves so their scent returns to normal and not rush the reintroduction.

You can also try calming treats or calming sprays to help matters along. If it's a persistent problem (totally been there—we feel you), talk to your vet or a feline behaviorist.

Cat Tale: A Tale of Eight Kitties

Cat writer Deb Barnes has always lived in multi-cat households and she's adept at helping the felines in her life adapt to changes in the home dynamic.

"I find that most challenges arise as the cats begin to age," she notes. "Personalities can change, or physical, mental, or dietary needs, which can result in rifts or shifts in the dynamic, which have to be adjusted accordingly to keep the peace—and [keep] everyone happy and healthy."

However, when a tiny black kitten, now named Shadow, showed up at her home in 2019, she and her seven cats were in for quite the challenge.

"We currently have two very strong adult alpha males in the mix, as well as one adult alpha female, who were already competing for

the top rung of the social hierarchy," Barnes says. "When [Shadow] appeared at our doorstep about a year ago at approximately six months of age, he was significantly younger than the other seven, set-in-their-ways cats, ranging in age from seven to fifteen years old. He disrupted the delicate balance with his energy and aggressive tendencies, and even though we did not rush the introductions, they did not take to him with the same relative ease I was accustomed to. So we had a substantial rise in catfights, bullying, and urine marking, even though all the cats have been spayed or neutered."

Barnes and her fiancé hadn't intended to bring another cat into the home, but after failing to find Shadow's owner and then learning that he'd been abused, they felt their home was the right one for the kitten. They began working with him to build trust and overcome his aggressive tendencies, and they saw progress as Shadow warmed to them.

The seven other cats took a bit more time to warm to Shadow, but Barnes helped them accept the new addition by considering the situation from a feline perspective and focusing on providing a safe and enriching environment for everyone.

"My solution revolves around thinking as if I were a cat," she says. "Cats are wild by their DNA and they need an environment suited to their natural predator instincts. Because they are subject to whatever indoor environment we create for them, it is essential for their physical health and mental well-being that they are provided with fun and stimulating challenges to reduce boredom, which in turn reduces catfights, strengthens relationships, and keeps their minds and bodies fit.

"It's usually the simplest of things they appreciate. If weather permits, opening a screened window for some whiffs of fresh air and bird/bug/lizard/squirrel watching is a great diversion from the everyday environment. I also like to reintroduce old toys as new with a spray or sprinkle of catnip to liven things up. A box is always a wonderful treat, too, and I'll keep empties in the garage to bring in for exploring when I feel the cats need something new to do. I also encourage as many group activities as possible that are associated with positive rewards, which strengthens the bonds and relationships. Beloved mealtimes are eaten together in the same room, and treats are given every night after vigorous rounds of playtime with interactive toys. Grooming is done with each cat on a weekly basis, again, followed up with yummy treats so they look forward to me pulling the brush or comb out of the pantry drawer and associate being near one another as something good. We also make sure there are plenty of high and low spots for the cats to lounge and nap, whether they decide to share the space or go it alone."

Barnes has clearly done a phenomenal job of ensuring that every cat has access to necessary resources so they don't feel threatened, but what about one of the most valuable resources of all? Her time and attention.

"It's important also to respect and enhance the relationships you have with each cat individually to let them know they are loved and important to you, their beloved caretaker, and that the pecking order of the other cats does not threaten that relationship," she says.

Because she knows her kitties so well, Barnes has worked out time each day to spend with each animal individually, based on their needs. For example, Shadow and Zee get Barnes to themselves at night, while Peanut has exclusive access to Barnes's lap while she's working during the day.

By ensuring that each of her eight kitties gets an equal amount of time and attention when they need it most, Barnes has helped her multi-cat household to function peacefully. Of course, navigating the needs, feelings, and hierarchy of eight felines can sometimes feel like the worst of times. But, luckily, Barnes is usually able to enjoy the best of times—and all the purrs and snuggles that come along with them.

Signs of Conflict among Cats

It's easy to spot signs of open conflict among cats. They might stalk each other, hiss, growl, or turn sideways and puff their hair up to make themselves appear larger and more intimidating. If neither cat backs down from these displays, the conflict may escalate into swatting, pouncing, wrestling, and biting.

However, it may be much more difficult to recognize signs of silent conflict among felines. Typically, the aggressor can be identified as the one that stares down the other cats, approaches them and doesn't back down, and blocks their access to resources. Often, the cat creating the conflict will use body language to intimidate by raising his hindquarters and the hair along the back and tail. There may also be some low, rumbling growls.

The aggressor may soon have to do nothing but stare at another cat from across the room or begin an approach to frighten the cat off. This often results in the intimidated cat or cats not having easy access to necessary resources, like food, water, and litter boxes.

Over time, the threatened cat will hide more frequently and spend less time in areas where the aggressor—and, often, the family—spend time. He may only emerge and receive attention from the family at times when the aggressor isn't around.

CHAPTER 10

"Purrfecting" PDA

Your POV: I love my cat so much and show it by hugging and kissing her.	**Kitty POV:** Being picked up, hugged, and kissed can feel threatening.

We'll be the first to admit that it's difficult to resist picking up a cat. From their whiskered noses and furry paws to their soft bellies and fluffy tails, they look like they were designed to be hugged and snuggled and showered with kisses. However, just because they look adorable doesn't necessarily mean they're inviting this kind of physical affection.

When you were a child, maybe you had a well-meaning but overwhelming aunt or grandparent who, much to your dismay, couldn't resist pinching your cheeks, mussing your hair, kissing your forehead, or wrapping you in a tight hug whenever the opportunity presented itself. Maybe you tolerated it to be polite or squirmed away with discomfort. Or perhaps you've had a date who thought it was acceptable to hold your hand, give you a hug, or even lean in for a kiss that you didn't want. Such an experience isn't just unwelcome—it can also make you feel unsafe and downright frightened.

"Consent is such an important concept for people to understand in how we relate to other people and in how we relate to cats," Hannah Shaw says. "If you want to have an interaction with your cat, then your cat has to want that interaction as well."

Recognizing that your cat is a unique individual with his own likes and dislikes and his own level of comfort with physical contact is essential. And too often we don't consider this from the very beginning of our relationship with our cats.

"I think a lot of people who want a cat actually just want a squishy stuffed animal they can squeeze while they sleep," Shaw says. "But when you get a cat, you're opening your home to a living, breathing, sentient, independent, feeling being who has their own personality, their own interests, and their own likes and dislikes. So to build your relationship, you have to get to know the cat, find out who they are and what they like, and then see where your desires and interests intersect. Because if you both want to lie on the couch and snuggle and watch Netflix, that's awesome. But if you want to snuggle and watch Netflix and your cat doesn't? Guess what? You're not doing that."

So next time you're tempted to pick up your kitty and show him just how irresistible you find him, pause for a moment and consider how you'd feel if someone did the same thing to you. After all, personal space and consent aren't concepts that are reserved for people alone—they should be present in our interactions with all creatures we love and respect, including the furry members of our families.

And in America, pets are truly part of the family. In fact, 95 percent of US pet owners consider their pets to be family members, and millennials, who make up the largest segment of US pet owners, at 35 percent, are waiting longer to have kids and often treating their pets as children. "Pets are becoming a replacement for children,"

San Diego State University psychology professor Jean Twenge told the *Washington Post* in 2016.

Given that we may view our cats as our children—and the fact that they're so fuzzy and adorable—it's only natural that felines bring out our maternal and paternal instincts, compelling us to pick them up and snuggle them. There's even science to back that up.

A 2014 Harvard Medical School study found that, on a neurological level, the love and affection we feel for our pets is strikingly similar to what we feel for human children. In the study, 14 mothers looked at photos of their own pets and children, as well as other people's pets and children. When they saw their own pets and kids, a brain region known as the substantia nigra/ventral tegmental area—a part of the  brain involved with bond formation—lit up. "Several previous studies have found that levels of neurohormones like oxytocin, which is involved in pair-bonding and maternal attachment, rise after interaction with pets," notes veterinarian Dr. Lori Palley, who coauthored the study.

However, while we may view our cats as babies, they don't see us as their parents. Sure, a lot of cats certainly enjoy being stroked and petted. And studies have found that some cats will even choose human interaction over food. But these are felines that have learned to enjoy this contact from a young age, typically between two and seven weeks old.

And while we may show our affection by picking our kitties up and hugging and kissing them, the reality is that cats are lifted off the ground naturally only shortly after birth (by their mothers) or if they're carried off by predators. So even if we expect cats to enjoy being held all the time, we shouldn't be surprised when a cat doesn't respond positively to it.

Such interactions, especially when forced, can actually stress cats, frighten them, and make them more likely to avoid us in the future. A feline struggling to escape your grasp can also prompt clawing or biting, and this reaction can potentially cause injury to the cat as well if he falls while attempting to extricate himself from your grasp.

"For some cats, you may see signs as soon as you pick them up that they're already doing the math of 'How do I get down?'" says San Francisco–based feline behaviorist Daniel Quagliozzi. "They are looking around, their tail might be swishing, and they get very rigid because they feel like they're being restrained or held against their will."

The truth is that, if actually given the choice, many cats would prefer never to be picked up at all.

Myth: All Cats Enjoy Pets and Snuggles

We all know people who are huggers, those touchy-feely individuals who embrace virtually everyone, and we also know people who prefer a bit more personal space and would likely shy away if someone attempted to throw their arms around them out of the blue. Just as every person has a different personality and different levels of comfort with physical touch, so does every feline.

For example, Lynn's cat Dezi loves to be carried around in her arms; however, he's not a lap cat. Roo, on the other hand, refuses to be held, but she loves to curl up on Lynn's chest and spoon with her at night.

"I'm not a huggy guy," says Quagliozzi. "I am not into that so much unless I know someone, and in this day and age, you have to be conscious of other people's personal space, so I think it is very much the same with [cats]."

Some breeds of cat, such as ragdolls, are known for their affectionate nature and for even flopping back and lying comfortably when held; however, not even all ragdoll cats universally enjoy being picked up and held.

Before picking up any cat, it's important to learn your cat's preferences to ensure that you're both safe and enjoy your interaction.

To Pet or Not to Pet?

Not sure if your cat is enjoying those rubs, pats, and scratches? Use this kitty translation guide to determine if your cat wants you to keep on petting or give her some distance.

"More Pets, Please!"

- Cat initiates contact.
- Tail is held high and may be gently moving from side to side.
- Cat is purring and kneading.
- You'll note the cat's relaxed posture and facial expression, and the occasional slow blink.
- Cat gives you a rub to initiate a pet or a nudge when you stop stroking her.

"Respect My Personal Space!"

- Fast-moving swishing, thrashing, or thumping of the tail
- Quick turn of the head to face you or your hand
- Ears rotated backward or flattened against the head
- Passively accepting pets with no movement, purring, or rubbing
- Sudden short bursts of self-grooming
- Biting, swiping, or batting at your hand

While cats do enjoy being up high, so they can gain a better view of their territory, there's a difference between a cat that leaps atop a bookshelf by choice and a cat that's scooped up into a person's arms. Domestic cats are unique in that they're both predator and, because of their small size, prey. So, for a feline, there's a great deal of security in having full control over their limbs and being able to run, jump, or hide at will.

Kittens may certainly be used to being scruffed by their mothers, but this often occurs only when the mother must relocate her young for protection. The only other time cats may be picked up is when they encounter a predator, such as a coyote or a bird of prey, so it's only natural for a cat to be stressed or frightened when she suddenly loses contact with the ground and her ability to escape is limited. For many cats, this may even be interpreted as an attack.

Snuggling simply isn't a normal form of interaction among felines. Cats show affection among their own species by head bunting, rubbing against one another, or grooming each other, and cats that are bonded may certainly cuddle together. However, outside of a mother relocating her kittens, felines don't pick each other up.

And while we may be comforted by a warm hug or a shoulder to cry on when we're frightened or upset, cats don't share this need for physical comfort. When they're stressed or scared, it's instinctual for felines to run away and hide or seek solace in a location far from the ground. So don't insist on snuggling a frightened kitty—odds are, you'll only exacerbate your cat's stress.

Being fearful of being picked up and cuddled may also be a learned behavior among cats. They may associate such interactions with negative experiences, such as transportation to the vet, being restrained to have their nails trimmed, or receiving vaccinations. Cats may also be wary of interacting with people, especially children and strangers, because of how people approach them. Both children and adults who are unfamiliar with cats may attempt to handle a cat against his will.

"Because of their lack of knowledge of cats, people are actually quite rude and impolite toward most cats," Dr. Tripp says. "Now the reason they are rude and impolite is because they think mistakenly that it's okay to approach and begin to stroke it without permission. That's like a guy thinking they can go up and hug any girl they want. It's not okay unless you're invited."

The key to giving and receiving physical affection with a cat is to give the feline as much choice and control during the interaction as possible. This means letting the cat decide if she wants to be petted, where she wants to be petted, and how long she wants to be petted. Generally, friendly, socialized cats enjoy being rubbed or scratched in the regions where they have scent glands, such as their cheeks, the base of their ears, and under their chins.

But keep in mind that just because a cat enjoys chin rubs one time doesn't mean she always wants them. You may also like to snuggle up to a loved one sometimes, but does that mean you're looking for a cuddle all the time? Probably not. So pay attention to the cues your kitty gives you to determine if she's enjoying your interaction. Is she purring and leaning into your hand for more, or is she merely tolerating the attention? Not all cats communicate by biting or running away, and cats that endure unwelcome physical attention experience higher levels of stress than ones that actively dislike petting.

So take Quagliozzi's advice and surrender your expectations about what should happen when you interact with your cat. "My tagline over the years has become, 'Surrender yourself—not your cat.' This is an animal that you can't control, and you have to surrender to the fact that your cat needs every experience to go down by their own choice. Essentially, by doing less, by not trying to force your cat to live by your rules, you'll get more from your cat," he says.

Do's and Don'ts of Kitty Handling

DON'T insist on holding a squirming cat that's struggling to get away. This will only make it more difficult to pick up your cat in the future, and it may make him afraid of you.

DO approach your cat so that he's aware of your presence before you pick him up. Approaching your cat from behind may startle him.

DON'T cradle your cat like a baby. While some felines may be comfortable in this position, most don't like being placed on their backs because that makes them feel vulnerable.

DO place your cat down gently onto the floor, a table, or another safe surface and allow your cat time to regain his footing. While you may have heard the saying that cats always land on their feet, don't drop your cat or let him leap from your grasp, as this could injure both of you.

DON'T scruff your cat. Leave that to mother cats and don't force your cat into this position.

Can Cats Be Taught to Enjoy Cuddles?

Some cats may feel right at home snuggling up in your arms, but if your relationship with your kitty is more of a hands-off one, can you change that? It's possible.

If your cat isn't a fan of public displays of affection, you may be able to get your cat more comfortable with such interactions. However, it's important to respect your cat's boundaries and understand that many cats, especially older ones who may not have been socialized much as kittens, may never be comfortable being picked up, held, or even petted. Be sensitive to your cat's tolerance levels for this kind of interaction, and respectful of the fact that being held may make your cat feel unsafe or uncomfortable.

"There are just some cats that will never ever want to do that, and that's where respect comes in," says Quagliozzi. "That's where you have to just say, 'Aw, shucks, I have this cat that does not want to be handled and that is just who they are.'"

However, with time and patience, many cats can become accustomed to—and even enjoy—physical affection. The trick is to take it slow and let your cat initiate contact.

"The proper way to greet a cat is to extend one finger out toward the cat, but stop an inch away from their nose," Dr. Tripp says. "That last inch is the cat's decision. The cat then either backs away or comes closer and sniffs. This smallest presentation of your scent and the cat can take it in. Then, if the cat decides that they are okay with you, they move forward and bunt, and put their cheek scent on the end of your finger. That is like permission. 'Yes, I will put

my scent on you first. Now you can put your scent on me.' Then they'll rub against you and allow you to begin to stroke them. And they'll often communicate then through purring and through seeking attention."

Dr. Tripp also suggests trying hand-feeding to help a cat warm up to you. "Start with tossing food at a distance and then just get closer and closer," he says. "Feeding gets your scent onto the food."

If your cat is comfortable with petting, but is hesitant to be picked up, start by simply placing your hand on your cat's side and immediately releasing, and gradually work your way up to placing hands on both of your cat's sides. Do this several times before attempting to pick your cat up, and be sure to praise your cat and reward her by playing with a favorite toy or giving her a delicious treat. The first few times you actually pick your cat up, keep it short. Pick her up, hold her gently yet securely close to your chest, and promptly put her back down. With consistent practice—and plenty of positive reinforcement—some cats may get accustomed to being held for short periods.

"It may take some experimentation and a little bit of trial and error," says Quagliozzi, who notes that his own cat took some time to warm up to physical affection. "In the beginning, my cat was aloof, wouldn't even sit next to me, and would try to bite me when I went to pet him. That was when we first met, but where I am now, I can cradle my cat in my arms for five to ten minutes sometimes."

Kitty Care: Eight Ways Cats Say, "I Love You"

Purring: While purring doesn't always indicate contentment—cats also purr when they're injured or scared—it's often a sign of a happy cat.

Grooming: When your kitty licks your arm or grooms your head, she's mingling her scent with yours and marking you as part of the family.

Slow blinks: If your cat gazes at you while slowly blinking, it's a sign than he's very comfortable with you. Slow blinks are even called "kitty kisses."

Tail position: A tail held high in the air or curved like a question mark is a sure sign that your cat is happy to see you.

Kneading: Kittens knead their mothers' bellies to stimulate milk flow, and cats that continue to knead while snuggled up with you are expressing their contentment.

Staying close: Even cats that don't enjoy physical affection will show they care by simply hanging around you, sleeping next to you, or following you from room to room.

Head bunts and leg rubs: Cats have scent glands in their cheeks, so when a cat rubs against you or offers you a head bunt, they're showing affection and marking you as their own.

Belly exposure: Rolling over and showing you their vulnerable belly doesn't necessarily mean a kitty wants a belly rub, but it does indicate that a cat is extremely comfortable around you.

Cute Enough without a Costume

We've all seen the photos of kitties on Instagram wearing ridiculous hats or dressed as pirates or tacos for Halloween. These felines may look adorable, and, sure, many of them may even tolerate the costume, but, for most cats, being forced into clothing or a costume isn't just uncomfortable—it's also downright stressful because it's wholly unnatural.

"When we start dressing cats to look like babies, it can become easy for us to miss the fact that the cat is becoming stressed or even depressed," says cat behaviorist Pam Johnson-Bennett. "Cats are not human babies, nor are they furry accessories. Cats may tolerate having costumes put on them, but many owners may not accurately read body language signals that indicate increased stress, discomfort, fear, or agitation. When I see many photos on social media of cats dressed up, I see stressed and sad faces, no matter how cute and funny the costumes may be."

As we've discussed, cats are prey animals that rely on their impressive senses to maintain awareness of their environment and keep themselves safe, but when a cat is wearing an outfit, both their movements and their senses may be compromised. A costume may make it difficult for a cat to easily walk, run, or leap, making her feel trapped and unsafe. It may also affect a cat's ability to see or hear, or it may squish her whiskers, which is uncomfortable and stressful.

"Cats rely on their ears, eyes, whiskers, paws, and fur to detect what's going on in their environment, and costumes can create a barrier so they can't navigate comfortably," says Johnson-Bennett. "Costumes that restrict the ears and also limit the cat's ability to use peripheral vision especially concern me. Cats are also sensitive to texture, and certain costumes can be very uncomfortable."

The scent of a costume may also trigger anxiety for felines. Cats rely on scent for identification and communication, so being covered in an unfamiliar smell can be unnerving, and it can also lead to aggression in multi-cat households, if another cat is unable to recognize the dressed-up kitty.

There's also the inherent danger of a cat chewing on pieces of the costume. Pieces that come off can be easily swallowed, which can cause choking or intestinal blockages.

So save the Halloween costumes for kids of the human variety, and instead show your kitty your love and affection with a little extra attention and playtime.

There's More Than One Way to Pick Up a Cat—But Here's What the Experts Recommend

As we've discussed, every cat has his or her own unique personality and preferences, which include how and when they like to be held. However, what's most important is for your cat to feel comfortable in your arms, so here are a few pointers to keep in mind:

- Always use two hands to pick up and hold a cat.
- Use one hand to support the cat's rear.
- Use the other arm to support the cat's chest in a way that allows her to rest in your arms.

CHAPTER 11

"Purrsonal" Space

Your POV: My cat hides because she's scared or unfriendly.	Kitty POV: I just want my own space sometimes. Don't you?

We've all experienced times when the world just gets to be too much. The introverts among us may feel drained after hours of making small talk at a party or overwhelmed and overstimulated from navigating noisy, bustling city streets. Even those of us who thrive on activity and love to be surrounded by others' energy sometimes need a break. We want a little privacy, we crave a reprieve from being "on," or we're just exhausted and need to curl up in a quiet place for a nap. And in this respect, once again, our cats aren't all that different from us.

But while we may retreat to the bedroom, the hammock in the backyard, or the living room couch to binge a favorite show, our feline friends often get a bit more creative when they want some alone time. They'll slip into the darkness and dust bunnies beneath the bed, scale the kitchen cabinets to observe the home from far above, or even squeeze themselves into spaces that don't seem remotely comfortable, like shoeboxes, bathroom sinks, and dresser drawers.

You may have noticed that your cat is likely to disappear at certain times of day—perhaps she slinks off to nap in her favorite secret spot each afternoon. Or it could be that specific situations prompt your cat to hide, such as when the doorbell rings, a friend comes over, or the kids get home from school.

Regardless of when or where your cat vanishes, though, there's no denying that felines are champions of hide-and-seek. What else do you call it when you frantically search for your kitty, while calling his name and rattling the treat container, only to discover him asleep inside a duffel bag atop a closet shelf?

What exactly is up with this behavior, though? Do our kitties just need a break from us? Are they truly scaredy cats? And does all that hiding mean that something is wrong? In this chapter, we'll seek out the answer to why cats hide and delve into ways to ensure that our felines' environment and our own actions provide our kitties with the personal space they need and crave.

Why Do Cats Love Boxes So Much?

Boxes are known as "cat traps" for good reason. Set one down in front of your cat, and your feline will very likely climb inside and claim it in a matter of seconds.

What makes boxes so appealing is that they offer kitties many of their favorite things. For one, there's a feeling of security when they're snuggled inside a box. They're protected on all sides, so a predator can't sneak up on them. Plus, they can hide while still keeping an eye on their surroundings so that no one can surprise them. And cardboard is also a great insulator, so it's a cozy, warm place for a catnap.

A simple cardboard box is essentially a safe space cats can retreat to, and research shows that boxes can actually help cats recover from illness faster and adapt to change more quickly. A University of Utrecht study observed a group of shelter cats that had just been introduced to a new environment. Half the cats were given boxes, and the other half weren't. The ones that were provided with boxes adjusted faster, exhibited fewer signs of stress, and were more likely to interact with people.

So keep a box on hand for your kitty to shelter in because it's much more to your cat than just a bit of cardboard.

Why Do Cats Hide?

Our feline friends seek out places to hide for a variety of reasons that are both instinctual and a response to their environment.

They need safety and security.

Felines are ambush predators, meaning they rely on stealth and strategy, rather than speed and strength, to capture their meals. They also have a unique place in the food chain because they're both predator and prey, so it makes sense that cats are masters at finding hiding places. To survive in the wild, they must be able to sneak up on prey, but they must also avoid becoming prey themselves. Sure, your indoor cat doesn't need to catch his own food or hide from coyotes, but the need to hide is instinctual, so most cats will hide.

"A hiding spot I think is vital for cats, even the easygoing kitties," certified animal behavior consultant Amy Shojai says.

"Lurking, stalking, hiding, watching for danger—or the rude dog—can be a self-preservation mechanism, or part of play. Giving cats a variety of resting spots gives them control over their environment, and boosts confidence. And a confident cat has less stress, and fewer health challenges related to stress."

Plus, since cats—especially indoor ones—spend much of their day snoozing, it's only natural to seek out a private place to nap where they're less likely to be surprised by a potential threat. Cats in the wild are constantly looking for "nooks and crannies to rest in because they want to have five sides out of six protected," cat behavior expert John Bradshaw told Catster.

And just because you can't see your cat doesn't mean that *he* can't see *you*. Many favorite feline hideouts, such as beneath the bed or atop a tall bookshelf, are those that allow your cat to survey his surroundings while going unnoticed. Cats often feel most secure when they're able to get up high and safely watch what's going on around them, which is why providing vertical space is so important.

They're stressed or frightened.

As we've established, cats are very sensitive creatures, so it doesn't take much to stress them out. "When cats are feeling stressed, they may seek out a small space where they feel safe, hidden away from any perceived threats, like a barking dog or the vacuum cleaner," says Kate Benjamin, cat style expert and founder of Hauspanther.com.

Moving to a new home or the arrival of a new pet or baby may prompt cats to start hiding more often. But so can the banging of a hammer when we hang a picture on the wall, the ringing of the doorbell on Halloween, strangers' voices, or the sudden dropping of a dish or another item. And some cats may also scurry away and hide at the onset of a stressor, such as a party full of loud guests or fireworks going off on the Fourth of July. They'll typically hide for the duration of the stressor—until the guests go home or the fireworks stop—and then emerge from their hideout.

Plus, felines in multi-cat homes may hide frequently if there's friction among them. Cats haven't developed conflict-resolution strategies, as some species have, so they may simply run away and hide to avoid potential interactions with an aggressor.

They need warmth.

You're already well aware that being warm is important to your cat. After all, how many times have you caught him soaking up rays in a sun puddle or stealing your recently vacated seat?

While your home may be warm enough for you, it's often not warm enough for your cat to be comfortable. As we noted previously, felines' thermoneutral zone, the temperature range necessary for them to maintain their core body temperature, is 86–97°F—about 20°F higher than ours. Meanwhile, the average temperature in most indoor cats' homes is around 72°F, according to the National Research Council.

So it's no surprise that our kitties seek out warm places to snuggle up in, often wedging themselves into small, enclosed spaces to help them conserve body heat. Some of their favorite hiding spots, such as cardboard boxes, provide insulation. And cats already often sleep in tight circles to conserve body heat, so a confined spot is the ideal way to curl up and catch some Zs.

They don't feel well.

When cats are sick or injured, they tend to hide as a survival instinct. After all, a weakened animal is more likely to become a predator's prey. Pregnant females also seclude themselves when they're about to give birth to keep both themselves and their young safe.

So while hiding is instinctual for cats, it can also indicate that something is wrong, which is why it's so important to understand what constitutes normal hiding behavior for your cat.

They just need a time-out.

We've all been there. Sometimes we just need a moment to ourselves, away from the computer, our phone, our children. So think of your cat's favorite hiding place as his own bedroom or meditation room. He needs a place to chill out and rejuvenate. Don't you?

Do This, Not That

DO create places to hide both high and low.

DON'T block your cat's access to places unless they're actually dangerous.

DO let your cat keep her hiding place a secret.

DON'T continually peek in at her, bother her, or attempt to remove her from her hiding place.

How much hiding is normal?

Cats are individuals, so while hiding much of the day may be normal for one, it may be highly unusual for another. No one knows your cat better than you, so when it comes to hiding, just keep in mind what's typical behavior for your cat.

You likely already have a good idea of what's normal for your house panther. You may know that she slinks off to the guest room every afternoon for a long nap or disappears into the box spring beneath your bed when the kids get home from school and the noise level increases. Perhaps you've even noticed that she hides more during the winter months, seeking out warm, cozy places in the sun or beside heating vents.

If the cause of your cat's hiding is part of her normal routine or can be linked to a stressor, like moving to a new home, the arrival of new upstairs neighbors, the introduction of another pet or a baby, the appearance of a houseguest, your new morning workout routine, or the fact that you're now learning to play the bagpipes, there's no cause for concern. Your cat simply needs some time to herself in a safe, quiet space, and she'll reemerge when she's ready.

However, if your typically social cat has taken to hiding frequently and you're not sure why, this may be indicative of another issue. Keep a close eye on her and look for any changes in her other behaviors, such as eating, drinking, grooming, and litter box habits, as well as her interactions with any other cats in the house. You may need to make a trip to the vet to get to the bottom of the problem.

Give your cat safe, snuggly hideouts.

As long as your cat seems happy and healthy, though, there's no reason to discourage her from hiding. Instead, provide her with the kind of hideouts she'd love to curl up in.

It's essential for your indoor cat to have a refuge, or an out-of-the-way spot where she can have some time to herself, as well as access to everything she needs, like food, water, a litter box, toys, and a scratching post. This could be an entire room of the house or even just a quiet nook, but it needs to be an area she can easily retreat to at any time. And when she's there, respect her choice and don't let other people or other pets bother her.

In addition to this refuge, your kitty needs plenty of hiding spaces. These can be anywhere your cat chooses—a closet shelf, a chair tucked under a table, a box in the corner of the room—as long as they're safe. Set up "purrmanent" areas where kitty can hide by placing blankets, boxes, and cat beds in particular areas.

For example, if your cat loves to snooze beneath the bed, make it cozier with a towel, a woolly blanket, or even a brown paper bag (cats love paper!). Or, if she enjoys observing the comings and goings of the home from atop the fridge, place a bed there, so she can snuggle up in comfort.

"The key is to provide cats with acceptable hiding spaces where they can go to feel comfortable, not hiding out in fear," Benjamin says. "Provide them with soft cave beds, decorative boxes, baskets, anything that allows you to see inside and easily reach inside for cleaning or if you need to retrieve your cat."

You can also regularly create new hiding places for your kitty, which is a great form of enrichment. Build a pillow fort on the couch, drape a blanket over a chair, or break out the scissors, tape, and your ever-growing collection of Amazon boxes and get crafty. It'll be fun for you, too!

However, cats aren't always the best judge of what spaces are safe to hide out in. (Has your cat ever climbed into a toasty-warm dryer? Not ideal.) So, in addition to providing plenty of great hiding spots, you may also need to deter your cat from crawling into some areas. Don't do this by forcibly removing him, shouting at him, or spraying him with water, though. Instead, restrict his access to these areas if you can by closing a door or rearranging the furniture. If this isn't an option, make the spot less appealing by spraying it with a scent he finds offensive, like citrus, peppermint, or cinnamon.

If your cat is hiding and you're not sure where she is, it's understandable that you may want to find her and make sure she's okay. But respect the fact that she's chosen to hide and get some alone time. After all, would you want to be disturbed when you're finally getting some peace and quiet?

"Take special precautions not to disturb your cat when they are curled up in a hideaway," Benjamin says. "This is their sacred space, and you don't want them to feel threatened."

Kitty Care: Hiding Spaces That Are the Cat's Meow

Provide plenty of places that tap into your cat's instinct to hide, including the following:

- Boxes
- Tunnels
- Cat caves
- Laundry baskets
- Suitcases
- Flowerpots
- Open drawers and closets (Make a habit of leaving these open, or check them thoroughy for a lounging kitty before closing them again)

CHAPTER 12

Outdoor "Pawsibilities"

Your POV: I'll never let my cat outside.	**Kitty POV:** I need more than these four walls. Can we compromise?

In the 19th century, urban populations grew exponentially and an increasing number of people moved into cramped, poorly ventilated spaces. These living conditions contributed to illnesses, and doctors began prescribing "natural disinfectants," such as sunshine and fresh air, to curb the spread of germs. As germ theory caught on and more medical professionals prescribed time outdoors, it drove reforms in US cities and led to improvements in housing ventilation.

In short, even a century ago, we knew that fresh air was important to our health. And today, evidence that we're healthier when we spend time in the great outdoors continues to pile up.

Fresh air and sunshine have been linked to lower blood pressure, less pain, faster healing, better mood, less anxiety, and even increased concentration. That's why doctors today continue to recommend outdoor time to patients. In fact, several states even have park prescription programs that empower doctors to provide free park passes to patients.

Clearly, access to the world outside the walls of our home is imperative to our mental and physical health. So it's not surprising that the same holds true for our cats.

We've already examined the multitude of ways that an indoor-only lifestyle can negatively impact our feline friends. In addition to the wealth of physical ailments associated with obesity and a lack of exercise, there's also the mental toll confinement can take, resulting in depression and anxiety that can manifest as undesirable behaviors. In fact, a 2009 study, published in *Applied Animal Behaviour Science*, analyzed more than 300 cats that presented with behavioral issues over an eight-year period and identified a lack of outdoor access as a risk factor for behavioral problems.

Perhaps it's safe to say that our cats also need a prescription for the great outdoors.

Most cat-owning Americans don't allow our pets fresh air and sunshine, though—and it's not to be cruel. We do it to protect our treasured four-legged family members. Indoors, we have more control over our cats' environment, so we can keep them safe from all the real and perceived threats of the outside world. We polled several owners of indoor cats and unearthed no shortage of dangers they'd worry about if their kitties ventured outside:

- Getting hit by a car
- Exposure to disease
- Being attacked by predators, such as coyotes, foxes, and hawks
- Fighting with other pets
- Getting lost
- Being harmed by neighbors
- Exposure to fleas, ticks, and mosquitoes
- Negative impact on local wildlife

In this chapter, we'll assess all the potential dangers that cats may face outside, using the latest data and research. And we'll delve into the multitude of ways that we can give our cats the fresh air and sunshine they need and deserve—and do it in the safest way possible.

Cat Tale: The Outdoor "Expurriment"

Richard Jung, editor of the cat-centric publication the *Purrington Post*, has long recognized the need for indoor cats to venture beyond the walls of their homes and engage with nature. However, the idea of letting his cherished pets explore on their own filled him with anxiety.

"Living in a more rural area, I always worried about my cats running off in an excited frenzy, chasing a field mouse or stalking birds, and getting lost," he points out.

But as Richard talked to his longtime friend Lynn and considered his cats' mental and physical health, he decided to let his pets outside in June 2020.

"I'd been told by Dr. Bahr that cats have a natural perimeter comfort level and rarely go more than a few hundred feet from their home," he recalls. "I was nervous but decided to do a controlled experiment."

Jung's cats, Mouse and Newman, now go outside every morning, and he always leaves a door open so they can come back indoors whenever they're ready.

"They love it," he says. "They get so excited each morning, and I'm thrilled to say we've had no issues or incidents. We have a country property and often spot them wandering around but always within sight of the house. I wish I had done this sooner. Their natural instinct to be outside and explore is exciting to watch, and their quality of life has improved greatly as a result. In fact, they're even more affectionate than usual. That's my experience and it has changed my understanding and behavior as a cat 'pawrent' for the better."

Living Nine Lives Outdoors

Although the majority of US cats never venture beyond the walls of their homes, there are millions of owned free-roaming felines here and across the globe. Now, we're certainly not saying you *should* let your cat free-roam. But what exactly do these cats do during the day? Where do they go?

If you've read any cat-related headlines in the past decade, you may assume that these outdoor cats are traveling miles every day on a bloodthirsty quest to wreak havoc on native wildlife. However, that's not only sensationalistic—it's also fundamentally inaccurate.

The Cat Tracker project, a six-year study that used GPS units to follow the movements of owned outdoor cats in several countries, found that most felines remained within 330 feet of their yard. And more than half stayed within 2½ acres (about two American football fields) of their homes. Only 7 percent of cats wandered more than 25 acres away from home. And most of these felines weren't exploring wild areas: 75 percent of them spent the majority of their time in yards and other human-modified locations.

Regardless of which country the felines resided in—from America to Australia—pet cats generally stayed close to home, which makes sense. These owned cats don't need to travel in search of their next meal since they're regularly fed at home. And because most pet cats are spayed or neutered, the animals also don't need to head out in search of a mate.

The study also found that male cats typically journey farther than females, younger cats more than senior cats, rural cats more than urban cats, and intact cats more than fixed ones.

As for what these cats do when they're roaming, a 2012 study by researchers at the University of Georgia sheds some light on the secret life of outdoor cats. Sixty cats in the suburbs of Athens,

Georgia, donned tiny cameras for the project, and every day, their owners downloaded the footage.

The findings were both amusing and illuminating. For instance, four of the cats were cheating on their owners with secret families, visiting neighbors' homes for snuggles and snacks. And many of the cats engaged in a variety of behaviors that their caregivers would probably prefer not to know about, including eating insects, earthworms, and roadkill, as well as exploring storm drains and drinking sewer water.

The most surprising discovery, though? Less than half of the participating cats (44 percent) stalked, chased, or killed prey. Those that did hunt preyed far less on birds than researchers expected. In fact, they mostly killed reptiles, a fact that Dr. Kerrie Anne Loyd, the ecologist who led the project, says other studies had overlooked because they didn't have the means to observe prey that was ingested or left behind.

These findings were shocking because, in recent years, outdoor cats' bird kills have been estimated to be in the billions, just in the United States alone. One of the most commonly cited papers, "The Impact of Free-Ranging Domestic Cats on Wildlife of the United States," authored by Scott Loss, Tom Will, and Peter Marra in 2013, acknowledges that most hunting is done by populations of feral, or community, cats as opposed to owned cats, which makes sense because owned cats are fed at home. However, the paper estimates that domestic cats kill 1.3–4 billion birds in the continental United States each year.

That's an astounding number of kills, especially considering that the Bird Conservancy of the Rockies' Partners in Flight Population Estimates Database estimates that there are only 3.2 billion birds in the entire continental United States. "The authors' 'conservative' estimate of birds killed by outdoor cats appear[s] to

exceed the total number of land birds estimated to be in the country," writes research and policy analyst Peter Wolf on his site, Vox Felina, where he analyzes research about outdoor cats. "According to the Partners in Flight Population Estimates Database—which, given its intended use for 'bird-conservation planning,' would seem to be the go-to source for the best estimates available—that total is 3.2 billion. That's only 33 percent greater than the median estimate (2.4 billion) developed by Scott Loss, Tom Will, and Peter Marra—leaving very little room for the many other sources of mortality,

Myth: My Cat Has No Interest in the Outdoors

Every cat is an individual, just like every person, and we all have different likes and dislikes. We all know outdoors-loving, granola-munching people who'd prefer to spend their weekends hiking and sleeping beneath the stars. And we all know people who'd consider a three-star hotel to be "roughing it." Our cats, too, may have similar feelings about the outdoors.

Maybe you've opened the door and given your cat the opportunity to explore the backyard, and he turned around and went right back to the couch. Maybe you tried to put a harness on your cat, and the experience left you both emotionally and physically scarred. Some cats simply won't be comfortable even sitting on your porch, especially if you live in a noisy or high-traffic area. That's okay.

But we'd bet your cat is still *intrigued* by the world outside the living room window. He still sniffs your shoes when you come home from a walk. He's curious about the birds and bugs that flutter by. He craves something new in his environment.

Even if your cat never roams the yard or naps in the catio, give him a taste of the sights, scents, and sounds of nature by regularly opening a window or bringing in outdoor items for him to investigate. We all deserve to explore and can benefit from making our worlds a little larger.

outdoor opportunities that allow them to enjoy the great outdoors while still keeping them safe. As we said before, it's not an either/ or situation. You wouldn't throw open the front door and let your toddler wander out to do as she pleased. Instead, you go outside with her, you make sure that a friend or family member keeps a close eye on her, you put her in a stroller, or maybe you even leash her. While you can certainly allow your cat to roam free if you decide that's what's best for him, you can also set these same kinds of boundaries with your cat to ensure that he's safe every time he steps outside.

But first, let's talk about deciding what kind of outdoor activity is right for your cat, as well as the steps you'll need to take to ensure that your indoor cat is prepared to venture outside the confines of those four walls he's so familiar with.

How Much Outdoor Freedom Should Your Cat Have?

The idea of letting your beloved feline outside—whether you give him access to the back porch or take him on leashed walks around the neighborhood—can be scary. We've already talked about the variety of threats facing a cat outdoors, and even if we've quelled some of those anxieties, you no doubt still have some concerns. That's okay. We do, too.

But often, we don't give our cats enough credit. They're smart, capable creatures that came from the outdoors, and it's only in recent decades that we've taken steps to fundamentally alter their lives.

"It's a pretty extreme concept to keep your cat indoors 24/7 with no access ever to feel the breeze on their face or the grass beneath their feet," says Hannah Shaw. "I'm not saying take your 12-year-old cat who's been inside their whole life and just put them outside on the Philadelphia sidewalk. Definitely not. But you can be protective of your cats while still respecting their individuality and understanding that they like the outdoors, too."

How can you do this? Start by assessing your cat as an individual. How old is she? What's her personality like? Is she skittish, or does nothing seem to rattle her? When she hears a sudden loud sound, like a knocking at the door, does she run away and hide or run toward it to investigate? Does your cat come every time you call? How does she react when she spots another cat through the window? Is she curious, afraid, aggressive?

Also, think about where you live. If you're in a suburban neighborhood or the country, you may let your cat roam a bit in the backyard on her own. If you live in a high-rise, on a busy street, or in an area with a lot of predators, you might not.

These are just a few things to consider, but no one knows your cat better than you, so use your best judgment when deciding how to give your cat outdoor access. If you live on a quiet cul-de-sac and have a feline that's not easily rattled and always comes when you call his name, you may be comfortable letting him explore the back patio on his own during daylight hours. If you have a fraidy cat or a kitten or a bit of a rebel who responds to his name only half the time, you likely won't give him that same type of freedom. He may be better suited to supervised porch time with you, a catio, or a leashed exploration of the yard.

It may be helpful to think of your cat as a child. (You probably already do that anyway.) A responsible, well-behaved teen is allowed more freedom than one who's immature or continually getting into trouble. And you'd give that teen more freedom, such as allowing her out on her own, than you would a five-year-old who requires supervision. As we've said again and again, every cat is an individual and has his own unique situation, so treat him as such. Not every cat should be permitted to roam free or even be allowed into the backyard without a watchful eye. But it depends on the cat and the boundaries you put in place.

"We want to show that a cat is capable of a lot more and can handle a lot more than we give them credit for," says Sandra Samman, who travels, hikes, camps, and even rock-climbs with her longhaired cat Denali. "Your cat will let you know what it is OK with. You can then push boundaries safely with your cat. Get in tune with your cat and you can show it the world."

Denali's adventures tend to be leashed ones, and he's a great example of how letting cats outside doesn't have to be a question of simply free-roaming or not. Even if you ultimately decide that Mittens can explore the backyard on her own, you should limit her outdoor time to when you're with her. And when it's time to come in, call her name and rattle that treat bag to entice her back in. Or, if you build a catio, for example, but live in an area with a lot of predators, you may let your kitty into his enclosure only when you're sitting right there with him. There are many ways to give your cat outdoor access and many steps and precautions you can take to keep your furry friend safe.

And just as you wouldn't let your kid spend the day on the beach without sunscreen or hand your teenager the keys to the car without first taking her to get a driver's license, you can prepare your cat to go outside. This can begin indoors by using positive-reinforcement techniques to ensure that your cat comes every time you call, or you may decide to leash-train your cat before going out. Also, it's imperative that your cat be microchipped and that he's been treated with parasite protection. And before he goes out, talk to your veterinarian about vaccines and other precautions you may need to take. In short, prepare your cat for outdoor adventures just as you would a child or anyone else you care about.

> "Get in tune with your cat and you can show it the world."

After all, why are you even considering letting your cat outside? Because you love your cat and want what's best for him, and, after reading this far, you know that outdoor access is essential to a cat's health and happiness.

"There is not really a replacement for outdoor enrichment," Shaw says. "You know, when I'm feeling stuck in quarantine, sometimes the only thing that can make me feel better is finding a wilderness area where I can go on a hike and feel the breeze in my hair and see plants and trees. These are all such important things that we shouldn't be taking away from a cat, especially a cat we say that we love."

Leashed Walks

If you're familiar with Adventure Cats, then you know there's no shortage of fearless felines traversing the globe, hiking trails, setting sail, and engaging in a variety of other activities that your average housecat isn't known for. The cats you'll find featured on AdventureCats.org and the @adventurecatsorg Instagram account all explore the world on leashes.

At first, it may seem strange—maybe even pretty off brand—for a cat to don a harness like a dog. Perhaps it just seems below a cat to be walked by a mere human, or maybe it's the fact that many people are quick to assume that felines can't be trained. Regardless, we hope that Adventure Cats has changed or will change your mind about what cats are capable of.

Now, that doesn't necessarily mean it'll be *easy*. Kittens are typically a cinch to get comfortable in a harness because they're young and open to new experiences. So if they're accustomed to being on a leash and exploring the yard, the neighborhood, or even a public trail from the beginning, they'll very likely always be as long as they get regular exposure to it.

Some cats even live a high-adventure lifestyle while on the safety of a leash, such as Denali. Denali has been in a harness since he was a kitten, and today Denali joins Samman on every kind of adventure imaginable, including rock-climbing expeditions.

"Denali is an extremely confident cat," Samman explains. "He loves to own any space he is in. He is curious and unafraid of most situations. Having safe outdoor experiences quells his curiosity. It

feeds his mind and soul. He soaks in so much. I couldn't imagine what he would be like if he only lived inside. I feel he would have pent-up energy and possibly take to bad home behaviors, like scratching furniture, which is something I don't deal with. He is fully stimulated by being able to go outside in a safe way."

For cats like Denali, the leash can be a ticket to a lifetime of travel and adventure. Denali goes virtually everywhere with Samman now, much like a gray tabby named Bug, who's often spotted alongside her owner, veterinarian Dr. Ken Lambrecht, sometimes leashed, sometimes not. In fact, Bug even splashes in waves at the beach and goes stand-up paddleboarding. "I had to step back from my training as a veterinarian, scientist, and wildlife biologist and just look at Bug in different terms," Dr. Lambrecht says. "She has truly opened my eyes to what cats are capable of."

And even older cats can take to a harness, such as Pan, a six-year-old orange tabby, adopted in New York City, who's lived in London, Edmonton, and now Vancouver. "Everywhere we go, we are always asked, 'How did you train your cat to walk like that?'" says Pan's owner, Rhiannon Lattimer. "The answer is that we let him call the shots. We started him out with walking, but he dictated at every stage how much or little he wanted. It just turns out, in our case, he wanted a lot. The biggest cat stereotype that I think we challenge is that *all* cats hate/fear change. Pan has traveled in cars, planes, trains, subways, buses, ferries, and in our bike baskets."

But your cat can be an adventure cat—and reap the mental and physical benefits of outdoor exploration—even if you never venture far from home. Take Figaro, a five-year-old black cat who lives in Chicago. Figaro started going on leashed walks with his owner, Anne Marie Klacko, when they lived in Texas, after he underwent perineal urethrostomy surgery for urinary blockages.

"We started taking Figaro for regular leashed walks after his surgery when I read that walks outside can be a good experience for cats with stress," Klacko says. "[It gives] them the exercise all cats need, [it gives] him one-on-one time with us in a multi-cat environment, and all that stimulation that comes with being outdoors [is] a satisfying experience for Figaro."

Figaro relished his time with his kitty caregivers and flourished in the great outdoors, even though he was never more than a few steps away from home. "Typically we just walk around the perimeter of our house," Klacko notes. "Figaro's leash and harness hang by our back door and he waits by it every morning. He likes to sit on the picnic table with me and sniff grass and trees. If he's feeling particularly energetic, we'll jog around the house. His walks and leisure time outside are anywhere between 5 minutes and 45 minutes."

So how do you leash-train a cat? Always start inside. Even though the goal is to get outdoors, it's important to ensure that your cat's harness is a good fit and that she's comfortable in it before you ever set paw outside.

As we've said, there are certainly some cats, especially kittens, who will take to a harness quickly. Some cat owners are able to put the harness on and their kitty is walking as if she doesn't even notice the new addition. However, most cats will need to adjust to wearing a harness, so begin by introducing it and creating a positive association with the harness. You can do this by letting your cat sniff the harness and providing her with a tasty high-value treat. You could also simply leave the harness by your cat's food bowl or feed her treats on the harness. Keeping the harness nearby during playtime or when your kitty is rolling in silver vine are other ways to start building that positive association.

The next step is to actually put the harness on. This can be a little unnerving for some cats because they're not used to wearing anything except their own fur coats, so don't force the harness on. Be gentle, talk in a soothing voice, and have treats or a favorite toy on hand to reward or distract your cat, if need be. Also, keep in mind that some cats may prefer different types of harnesses. One of Laura's cats doesn't like to wear a harness that slips over his head, so instead, he wears one that fastens around his neck and torso.

Once the harness is on, don't adjust it or tighten it just yet. Your cat needs to get used to the sensation of wearing the harness, so reward her with praise, treats, and playtime to continue that positive reinforcement.

Don't be alarmed if your cat freezes up, falls down, refuses to move, or walks strangely the first few times she dons her harness. Imagine if you suddenly had a harness strapped to your body. Wouldn't that take some adjustment? So entice your cat to practice walking in the harness by using food rewards and toys to get her moving. If she seems stressed, remove the harness, provide another reward to end on a positive note, and try again tomorrow.

Continue this process regularly until your cat is moving comfortably and you're able to adjust the harness for a good fit and attach the leash. This could take days or weeks—it just depends on the cat. But you don't want to rush the process or force your cat into a situation that makes her scared or uncomfortable. Not only could that make her fear the harness, but it could also make her fear you.

Once kitty is walking regularly in her adorable new harness and you've ensured that she can't back or wriggle out of it, it's time to go on your first outdoor adventure. Start somewhere close by, such as a yard, a courtyard, or a patio, and pick a time and location that's quiet and not heavily trafficked. You don't want your indoor cat's first foray into the backyard to be when your neighbor's dogs are barking or cars are honking nearby during rush hour.

"The most helpful tip I could give to those who wish to walk their cats after finding a harness that works for their kitty is the importance of finding the right type of space to let their kitty explore," Lattimer says. "Other friends tried taking their cats to open New York parks, and green spaces and just found that their cat just kinda sat there paralyzed. A cat, in this regard, is nothing like a dog. Cats need more enclosed spaces where they feel at ease to explore. Try finding a winding green path through some bushes or stick to the edges of parks. Your cat will thank you for it."

Pro tip: Always carry your cat out the door. This way, she'll get used to going outside only with you and won't learn to walk out on her own. If she gets used to walking out the door when her harness is on, she might also start walking out the door when her harness *isn't* on.

Now that you're outside, let your feline explore at her own pace. If she wants to immediately head into the shrubbery so she feels safe while observing this new environment, let her. If she wants to lie down in a sun puddle and nap, or snack on some grass, go for it. If she wants to dash right back inside, that's okay. It's important for your cat to take each step when she's ready. Forcing her to do something that frightens her will only backfire and make it unlikely that she'll want to try again.

It's also a good idea to bring along a familiar safe space for your cat to retreat to, such as a backpack or a carrier. But don't introduce it for the first time when your cat is also outside for the first time. Set it up indoors with a favorite blanket, some toys, and yummy treats, so she can get used to it.

Also, keep in mind that walking a cat on a leash is often quite different from walking a dog. While some cats will pull you down the sidewalk or hike for miles on a trail, most cats aren't so concerned with traversing distances. They'll want to meander, lie down in the sun, watch ants, stalk a squirrel, sniff the earth, and just breathe in the fresh air. You can certainly work with your cat to learn to follow leash commands, but remember that this outdoor time is for your cat. So don't be so concerned with the destination; instead, enjoy the journey—even if it only takes you a few steps away from the front stoop.

Depending on your cat's comfort level, you may soon be exploring much more than simply the backyard or the streets of your neighborhood. Waffles, a gray tabby who lives in Orange County, has been on a harness for her entire life, and she travels everywhere with her owner, Karen Nguyen. Waffles walks on the beach, hikes in the Colorado mountains, and paddleboards. She also rides on Nguyen's shoulder virtually everywhere she goes, whether it's to a local brewery or to make a Target run. And Waffles is a frequent flyer who strolls through airport security and prefers a window seat so she can watch the clouds pass by on her way to a new destination.

For more information on selecting the right harness and leash-training your cat, check out AdventureCats.org.

"Su-purr-vised" Outdoor Time

Plenty of cat owners let their cats into the yard, onto a porch, or out on a balcony, and simply keep a close eye on them as they wander and explore and, often, just nap nearby. Dr. Lambrecht even takes all four of his cats on half-mile off-leash walks through the woods.

As noted previously, the amount of freedom you give a cat outside should be based on the individual feline. If you're not sure how your cat will fare, provide her with an opportunity to venture out and see how she responds.

"Start slowly and never let them outside without supervision," says Pam Roussell, owner of the Purrrfectly Holistic cat boutique. "Make sure they know where their 'safe zone' or entry back in the house is so that, if needed, they always know where to go. Be patient—it takes time to build their confidence and understanding of their surroundings, but they absolutely love exploring new sights,

scents, and sounds. To watch the world through their eyes is fascinating and you can tell how much they are enjoying it."

Cats are smart. They know their names, and they'll often respond when we call them. At the very least, they'll respond to the crinkling of a treat bag or the sound of a can opening, right? And we can work with our cats to strengthen this behavioral response and teach them to come every time we call. So if kitty gets too close to the backyard boundary we've established or seems to be calculating a leap to the railing, we can call them back just as we would a human child in our care.

And as we watch our cats explore and interact with the environment, we may learn that some do just fine on their own while others may require a bit more restriction. "We started without harnesses, but due to the curiosity of one kitty, Gunner, in particular, the decision was made to start using [a] harness," Russell says.

Even if your cat's outdoor domain is limited to a small courtyard or an apartment balcony, it's still a whole new world for an indoor cat. And there's plenty to watch and hear, not to mention the multitude of scents that waft in with the breeze. "Coco just wants to sit on the patio furniture and feel the breeze, so more power to her," says Shaw, whose cats are leash-trained. "I'm not going to deny her that happiness."

Plus, you can make the area even more feline-friendly by setting up a chair, cushion, or perch for your cat, or bringing out some toys. But you certainly don't have to—your cat will find the places she loves, and she'll certainly create her own toys out of twigs and fallen leaves.

Leaves are actually 10-year-old Piper's favorite thing in the world, according to her owner, Rose Rosenhauer. "As the alpha of our household, Piper is a pretty serious cat, so I was overjoyed to see how playful she became when we discovered her love of fallen leaves," Rosenhauer notes. "On weekends, we let her on our balcony to enjoy 'her leaves.' She loves to joyfully roll in them and bat the leaves around. Fall is her favorite season."

Piper is proof enough that even a brief jaunt outdoors is all it takes to bring a little joy into an indoor cat's life.

Kitty Care: Apartment Dwellers Need Fresh Air, Too

Just because you live in a condo or an apartment doesn't mean that your kitty can't enjoy the great outdoors. You can open windows, install window perches, or kitty-proof the porch or balcony. You can also let your cat walk the apartment hallway, investigate the staircase, or explore other areas. And apartment kitties can even venture outside on a harness and leash, in a backpack, or in a stroller.

Strollers and "Catpacks"

We've done a lot of comparing cats to kids in this book, and we're not going to stop now. So while it may seem like pushing a cat through the neighborhood in a stroller, as you would an infant, is the ultimate crazy cat lady move, so what? Plenty of cats would enjoy some new scenery, even if they would never be comfortable walking vast distances on a leash. But you can "allow them to see the world—and do it safely—with a pet stroller," according to pet writer Sandy Robins.

The sight is becoming much more common. Just check out the #catstroller hashtag on Instagram. From the sidewalks of Toronto to the trails of Tennessee, cats are getting out and about in their own wheels more and more. Dr. Jennifer Stokes, DVM, clinical professor at the University of Tennessee's College of Veterinary Medicine, has even run a 5K with her cat Simon in a stroller. And stroller rides, along with leashed walks, are a common enrichment activity for the feline residents of Best Friends Animal Society's Kanab, Utah, sanctuary.

Denver resident Ashley McFarland takes her cats, Indie and Binx, on regular stroller rides around the city. "Indie and Binx really love going outside. You can tell they enjoy getting out of their routine—new smells, new animals," McFarland says. "The stroller was the first item I bought because they could both go in it and it seemed like a much smoother ride for them. I could also watch them and not have them facing away from me. I preferred the large jogging tires as they make for a smoother ride. I think this is important to make them as comfortable as possible and make it as positive an experience as you can. They actually sleep in the stroller almost every day when it's at the house, so I leave that stroller open and available for sleeping."

But if a stroller isn't for you, consider a backpack. "I think backpacks are a great option to bring along on walks, just in case you need to gain control of a situation," McFarland says. "They are a good solution for kitties that like to [go for a] walk and not be held, like Indie."

There are variety of cat backpacks on the market today. Again, not every cat will be comfortable in one. The confined space and the motion of riding around on someone's back may not be your cat's "purrfurred" way of adventuring, but for cats that take to it, the places they can visit is limited only by the imagination—or, you know, local laws and ordinances about where pets are permitted.

Catios

Outdoor enclosures for felines are called "catios"—essentially, patios for cats—and you've no doubt seen some jaw-dropping, envy-inducing ones that you'd love to have at your own home, if only you had the space, skills, and/or salary to afford such a catio. But while we certainly appreciate these gorgeous handcrafted structures with their multiple levels, ramps, and tunnels, unfortunately these catios just aren't in the cards (or in the budget) for most of us.

However, you have so many other options. There are pop-up tents of varying sizes that can easily be set up in a yard, in a park, or on a balcony, and you can find numerous detailed blueprints and catio plans available online if you're looking for a DIY project. And you can also simply get crafty.

Evan Griffith transformed the balcony of his Austin, Texas,

apartment into a catio for his cat using chicken wire. He covered all sides of the area and secured it by stapling the wire to the roof and floor of the balcony and tying the sheets of wire together at the edges. Lots of cat owners have taken this approach, enclosing decks, porches, patios, and even pergolas with lattice, chicken wire, or other materials to keep cats safely inside.

"I turned my apartment balcony into a catio because I wanted my indoor cat, Kylie, to have a taste of the outdoors in a safe way," Griffith says. "She absolutely loves it and spends much of each morning and evening out there, basking in the sunlight and lurking

among the fronds of my Boston fern, a cat-safe plant. Access to the balcony seems to have alleviated her apartment restlessness—I've noticed improvements in her mood and energy."

Corey Wright did something similar for her cat, Fray, in her previous apartment, kitty-proofing the balcony so that Fray could lounge outside under her watchful eye. "I knew pretty quickly that Fray wanted to go outside," she says. "The patio was the best option because I could make it safe and he'd have space. He *loved* it out there. He would go to the door every morning and meow to be let out. He would watch birds and squirrels and other animals in the complex. But his favorite was just rolling around, getting all the outdoor smells on him. He would hate when I came out to get him."

Want to build your own catio? Crafty kitty caregivers often go green and repurpose materials to create their own version of a

catio. For example, Cynthia Fuller's cat, Casper, relaxes inside a window-mounted enclosure created from items her family already had. "My husband built our catio out of repurposed materials from a chameleon enclosure he built for our son several years ago," explains the North East, Maryland, resident. "He used scrap wood and screen that he stapled to the frame. The floor is made out of a pallet that he brought home from work."

A simple catio can also be constructed from a pet crate, as Skylar Pratt of Buffalo, New York, did. "Get a large dog crate and

Do This, Not That

DO look for ways to let your cat outside.

DON'T let your cat out when you're not home.

DO make sure that your cat has a breakaway collar with tags and a microchip.

DON'T let your cat out without identification.

DO let your cat out only if you trust him and feel confident in your decision.

DON'T let a scared, timid, or new-to-the-home cat outside.

DO install cat-proof fencing, just as you'd fence in a yard for a dog.

DON'T let your cat roam your neighbors' yards without permission.

two L hooks," he says. "Hang the dog crate off the two L hooks that you put in the outside wall of the house or apartment at a height where the bottom of the crate can rest on the windowsill. If there is not enough security, you can add a piece of wood like a 2×4 under the crate and screw that to the wall/crate for added support."

Pratt further outfitted his cats' dog crate–turned–window perch with holes for drainage when it rains and an outdoor carpet for style and comfort.

Space is often a concern with catios, but many of these solutions don't take up much room or simply fill available space you already have. And if you want to build a roomier catio, but don't have space to expand outward, you can always build *up* instead.

"We didn't have a lot of room on our back patio, so we had to make the best use of the space that we had," Holli Johannes of Portland, Oregon, said. "The catio extends all the way to the ceiling and has staggered shelves covered in outdoor carpeting that are big enough for [our cat] to lie on. We covered the outside with wire to keep him contained. We also added a human-size door with a latch so that we can get in there and clean. All told, it cost us less than $100."

No matter what kind of catio space you create, your kitty is sure to enjoy a little sunshine and fresh air. And you can further enhance this outdoor space by creating opportunities that your cat doesn't often get inside. For example, even if you're on a small balcony, you can collect rocks, twigs, acorns, and leaves for your cat to sniff and swat around. Wright keeps a small children's pool with a few inches of water on her balcony because Fray loves to bat toys around in the water and settle inside it to cool off on hot days.

"The pool was added when the temps rose a bit," she says. "He loves water, so I put a shallow amount in there so he could climb in and out, splash around, drag his toys in. Sometimes he'd just sit in it."

Construct a window box for $35

You can create a simple and safe outdoor spot for your kitty that won't break the bank—or take more than an hour to construct.

Supplies:

- Two 6-foot wire shelves
- Hacksaw, bolt cutters, or another tool to cut wire shelves
- Zip ties
- EZ cable clips
- Four 1¼-inch deck screws
- Screwdriver or drill
- Level
- Tape measure
- Marker or pen to mark where to cut shelving

Directions:

Measure the width of the window where you'll place the box. (We recommend a window in a room where you spend a lot of time, such as an office or living room, so that you can keep an eye on your cat when she's in the box.)

Cut one of the wire shelves into two panels that are the width of your window. (In our example, we created 32-inch pieces.) Cut the remaining shelf into another panel of the same length. These will be the top, bottom, and front of the box.

Cut two pieces from the remaining piece of shelving that are half the size of the longer panels. (In our example, we cut two 16-inch pieces.) These will be the sides of the box.

Take two of the longest panels and position them (longest sides together) to form an L shape. Secure the corners together with zip ties, as illustrated.

Attach one of the short shelving pieces to one corner of the L-shaped piece with zip ties, as illustrated. This forms one side of the box. Repeat on the other end with the second 16-inch piece.

Attach the remaining long panel to the top of the contraption with zip ties so that it forms a box with one open side, as illustrated.

Now that the box is complete, it's time to attach it to the window.

Have one person hold the box up to the window and ensure that it's level. Next, use the cable clips and screws to attach the box to the outside of the window in each of the four corners.

Ensure that the box is sturdy and tightly secured so that it can hold your cat's weight.

Place a mat, piece of carpeting, or another material in the bottom of the crate so kitty will be comfy.

Open the window and let your cat out to safely enjoy the sunshine! Remember to only let your cat into the box when you're nearby to supervise.

CHAPTER 13

A Dream Home from a Cat's "Purrspective"

Your POV: My cat has everything he needs indoors.	Kitty POV: Oh, I could think of a few more things . . .

We've all seen those gorgeous kitty dream homes with the staircases and climbing posts that lead to elevated walkways with bridges and tunnels to every room. And we've coveted those feats of feline architecture while also accepting that we will likely never reside in such a feline-friendly space because constructing it requires both skills and funds that we just don't have. But the good news is that you don't need to build a kitty "purradise" in your home, nor do you need to let your house go entirely to the cats, to create a space where your feline friend will thrive.

"Environmental enrichment doesn't have to be expensive or complicated," says Kate Benjamin, whose website Hauspanther. com showcases how cat owners' homes can be stylish as well. "'Catification,' as Jackson Galaxy and I define it in our books, is the art of designing your home to accommodate your cat's environmental needs, as well as your own aesthetic and functional desires. In other words, you can give your cat what he or she requires to thrive without sacrificing your own sense of style or comfort—or your bank account. This way everyone is happy and at ease. And keep in mind that you can start small and keep adding new elements. Just pay attention to how your cat is using the space and experiment."

Speaking of space, let's start there and take a look at what our feline friends require.

Vertical Space

Space is important. It's why we'll pay more for a first-class or a business-class seat on a plane if it's within our budget. It's why we feel a sense of relief when we leave a cramped dorm or hotel room. Being able to stretch and move and get away from the confines of our physical space—and the people we share them with—is essential to our health and well-being.

It'll come as no surprise, then, that our feline friends need space, too. Cats' wild and free-roaming counterparts have unlimited space. And even owned outdoor cats that may not venture too far from home at least have the choice to explore far and wide. Indoor cats, though, have only the square footage contained within four walls. And the same goes for you. Heck, you'd love to have a larger kitchen or a spare bedroom, right? But you have to work with what you've got. Luckily for your cat, you don't need to expand outward—you can create more space simply by expanding upward. "One thing every cat owner should keep in mind is how they use their physical space and even their furniture to create vertical space for their cats, particularly with regard to access to windows," Kitten Lady Hannah Shaw says.

Since cats are both predator and prey, they are constantly surveying their surroundings.

You may have constructed a lofted bed in your college dorm room to open up floor space, and this is exactly what you can do for your kitty. It's called "vertical space," and it's essential for indoor cats. "It's important to give cats places to climb that allow them to get up off the floor," Benjamin says. "Since cats are both predator and prey, they are constantly surveying their surroundings, looking for threats and potential prey. Being up high allows them to get a better view. Cat trees, perches, shelves, windowsills, etc. can all serve this purpose. Keep in mind that climbing includes all levels of vertical space, from just off the floor to way up high and everything in between."

You're likely already aware that your cat desires a high vantage point. It's why your cat hangs out atop the kitchen cabinets, the bookshelf, the refrigerator, or any other tall object she can scale.

(It's why Laura's cats sometimes drape themselves on top of the bathroom door, even though they have plenty of vertical space options throughout the house. Show-offs.)

Creating these elevated vantage points can be as simple as purchasing a cat tree or moving a piece of furniture near a bookshelf, so kitty can safely and easily reach the highest point in the home. "Cats really want to be able to access high points safely, and if you don't give them a chance to do it safely, they're going to do it unsafely anyway," Shaw points out.

You can even make these high-altitude escapes more appealing by placing a cat bed or towel atop them, creating a cozy place to nap. But there are countless other ways to enhance the vertical space within your home. You can add perches to windows or shelving to the walls. There are climbing frames, raised walkways, hammocks, platforms, and more.

Not sure where to place a perch or what kind your kitty might enjoy? Let him tell you. Just pay attention to the areas he's repeatedly trying to access or the places where he's already curling up for a snooze. He's showing you where he wants to be and where he's already comfortable enough to settle in for a catnap.

And while you could certainly spend a fortune on designer cat-friendly home décor, there's no need to break the bank. Just get creative. Move furniture around so your cat can access the high points in the home or play her very own version of The Floor Is Lava. "Cats love to be able to circumvent a room without touching the floor," says Jodi Ziskin. "So a tower, some shelves, and access to the couch and coffee table create a kitty superhighway."

You can also use spare wood or pick up some IKEA shelves and transform a blank wall into the ultimate kitty climbing wall. Position a cat tree in the corner of the room—or construct your own carpeted climbing post, leading to a perch, shelving, or rafters high above your head.

And just because you make your home more appealing and enjoyable for your kitty doesn't mean it has to detract from the overall style of your interior space. There are countless aesthetically pleasing, cat-friendly home décor options on the market today, and just as many "hacks" that are only a Google search away.

Horizontal Space

You've likely heard the case for vertical space before, but horizontal space is just as critical. Yes, cats love a high space from which to survey their kingdom, but they also need floor space where they can sneak away, monitor their surroundings, and, of course, curl up for a nap. Luckily, there are many ways you can provide this type of space without giving up your own floor space.

For one, don't block cats from getting under the bed. We've already established that cats need places to hide, so let them crawl into this private space that so many of them love.

Identify floor areas that could make excellent hiding places, such as behind the curtains or beneath a chair, and place a cozy cat bed or old towel there to encourage your feline friend to take a load off.

Don't shut all the closet doors—give cats access to these quiet retreats. This is exactly what Corey Wright did for her cat, Fray, when she discovered that he loved the bedroom closet in her previous apartment. "The closet was a go-to retreat for him since the day I brought him home," she recalls. "It's quiet and cool, and he loved to just hang out back there. I would toss a fleece blanket back there so he could burrow or make a nest. I would peek to make sure there's where he was sometimes, but always let it be his special place." Just be sure that closet is kitty-free before you shut the door.

And try opening a bottom drawer, so kitties can tuck themselves away for a catnap. Sometimes nestling among socks or sweaters can be the ideal hideaway. And, come on, it's not like your clothes aren't already covered in cat hair anyway. Again, be careful not to close a drawer while your kitty is napping inside.

Their Own Space

When you share a living space with someone—whether it's a room-mate, a dormmate, or even your own child—you find ways to share the home, while also ensuring that you each have your own personal space. Cats deserve the same. You may not be able to give Mittens her very own room, of course. (Although she'd surely appreciate it if you did.) But there are ways you can give cats ownership over their environment just as you would when you share living space with a fellow human being.

For one, make sure that every room of the house has a space that's designed just for Mittens. This could be a cat tree to scratch and climb or a bed or blanket atop the living room bookshelf. It could be a window perch or a cardboard box nestled in the corner. Just as you and your roommate merge your furniture and belongings together in common spaces, you can do the same with your feline friend's belongings—even if you are the one who has to "purrchase" those belongings.

But cats also need their own spaces. As we discussed in a previous chapter, they require hiding places to get away, rest, and observe, and they also need a refuge, a space where they can access everything they need (food, water, litter, toys, scratching post) and not be bothered by other people or pets in the house.

Veterinarian Dr. Ken Lambrecht even created an entire playroom for his cat Bug, which he named Bug's Gym. "It started with building Big Mountain [a large mountain for Bug to scale]," he said. "Then I added running wheels, climbing walls, and everything else. It is important we tend to the needs of cats to climb, hide, and, generally, be active and stimulated in their indoor environment."

Cats also crave plenty of cozy places to nap. "Give your cat plenty of soft beds or blankets where she can rest comfortably," Benjamin says. "These soft materials will absorb her scent, adding to her sense of ownership and ideally putting her at ease. Also, by giving your cat designated places to nap, you can help to contain the cat fur, keeping it off your furniture. Consider placing at least one comfy bed in front of a window so kitty can watch the activity outside."

Warmth

As we noted earlier, felines' body temperature is about 20°F higher than ours, which is why the indoor home environment is often a little chilly for our kitties. So provide areas where your cat can warm up.

Every cat loves a sun puddle, so this could be as simple as opening the curtains or blinds so cats find sun-soaked patches of carpet. But you can also provide cozy beds, blankets, or towels to nestle into, and even cardboard boxes, which offer great insulation.

There are also plenty of heated beds, mats, and perches on the market. The most coveted catnapping spaces in Laura's home are the heated window perch with a birdfeeder outside and the heating pad set to low and covered with a blanket that's tucked into a nook of the cat tree. In the winter months, especially, we'll always find a couple of cats cuddled up and snoozing away in these locations.

Quiet

Cats have remarkable hearing. They can detect a wide range of frequencies and hear higher-pitched sounds than humans and even most

dogs. Their already sensitive hearing is further enhanced by their movable ears, which amplify sound and enable felines to discern which direction a noise is coming from.

This excellent hearing is incredibly useful in the wide-open spaces of the outdoors, allowing cats to hear a variety of sounds and easily detect where prey is hiding. However, sound reverberates differently inside. It's why teachers advise children to use their "indoor voices" and why movie theaters can sometimes be uncomfortably loud.

So just imagine what that blaring television or stereo sounds like to your cat. Or the roar of the vacuum. The grating of the garbage disposal. The screams and stomps of playful children. It can easily become too much for you. But for a cat, it's even louder and can often become downright frightening.

It's something even we hadn't considered much before we noticed how shelter cats would cringe each time a door was slammed shut. But think about the times you've been overwhelmed by noise: the blare of a fire truck passing you in the street, the house party down the street that continues late into the night, the incessant crying of your neighbor's infant at 3 a.m., and more. Consider the stress associated with these events. They may be short-lived, like the siren, resulting in a brief surge in adrenaline, or they may last for hours or days on end, slowly wearing away your patience. So what must the noisiness of indoor life be like for the felines we share our homes with? And how must that affect their health?

Little to no research has been done on the effect of sound on indoor cats (you might even say that researchers are pretty much silent on the topic—pun intended). But it's certainly possible that cats are living in homes that expose them to chronic noise they find aversive.

We can't keep sound out of our homes. (With three cats and a dog, Laura understands the value of a vacuum cleaner.) But what we can do is simply be more aware of the aural disruptions that we allow into our cats' environments. We can turn the music down. We can open the trash bag a bit more quietly. In other words, we can try to be more respectful of our feline roommates, just as we would show respect for our human ones.

Places to Scratch

We know that scratching is a natural behavior for cats. It's how they communicate—both visually and pheromonally—mark their territory, stretch their muscles, and remove the outer layer of their claws. If we don't provide them with appropriate places to engage

in these behaviors, cats will find their own, whether it's the living room rug or the side of your favorite recliner.

And just one scratching post or cardboard scratcher won't do. You don't have just one place to sit in your home, do you? Give your cat options as well by placing scratching opportunities in various rooms. "You need a scratcher in every room, and there's no excuse not to," Adelman says. "Once upon a time, all cat trees were like crazy cat lady ugly furniture. But now you can get really nice ones."

As we noted before, you also need to provide materials and ways to scratch. "Try different kinds of scratchers with a variety of materials, including carpet, rope, woven sisal, wood, cork, etc. to see which your cat prefers," Benjamin says. Also consider the orientation of the scratching surface—horizontal or vertical. Some cats may prefer one over the other. And finally, the location of the scratchers is critical for getting your cat to use them. Try placing them in areas where you spend the most time, since your cat will want to leave their scent in these places."

Scratchers and vertical space can also fulfill two feline needs. For example, a carpeted tower or cat tree offers an elevated escape, as well as plenty of real estate for kitties to sink their claws into.

Litter Boxes

Litter boxes are a lot like cats themselves: You can never have too many of them, right? Sure, your partner, your landlord, or even society at large may disagree, but, to your cat, one litter box often just isn't enough.

More than one litter box? That can sound like too much to even the craziest of crazy cat people, but wouldn't you rather your kitty have multiple boxes, rather than finding his own alternative elsewhere in your home?

So to ensure that your cat will use the litter box(es), consider not only the number of boxes, but also the type. "Decorative litter hiders and covered litter boxes can make the litter box more attractive, but not every cat will be comfortable using one," Benjamin points out. See how your cat interacts with the box. Does he walk right in, circle it, balance on the edge of it, keep his head outside while he uses it? Also, consider how the location of the box or the type of litter you provide may affect your cat's litter box experience. Our felines are always communicating with us—we just need to pay attention. "Make sure you listen to what your cat is telling you with his or her behavior," Benjamin notes.

A common cat owner complaint about litter boxes is the smell, but cats have the same complaint. They don't want to use a stinky, messy toilet any more than we do. The solution is simple: Keep it clean. This may require scooping it out multiple times a day, but both you and your cat will appreciate the effort—and it'll save you additional cleanup time if kitty decides to create her own litter box.

"The necessary evil of living with cats is the litter box, but this doesn't have to be a burden for you or an unpleasant experience for your cat," Benjamin adds.

A Bit of the Outdoors

Even if your indoor cat never sets paw outside the home, you can and *should* create enrichment opportunities by bringing the outdoors in. This can be accomplished in a multitude of ways. Here are just a few:

- Open a window.
- Provide grass or safe edible plants.
- Pile up brown packing paper so your cat can root around and rustle in it, as they would outdoors with leaves.

- Bring objects inside, like sticks, small rocks, acorns, and leaves for your cat to sniff and investigate.
- Place a tray of dirt in the bathtub and allow kitty to sniff, dig, and even roll around in it, if he chooses. (Don't worry—he'll give himself a bath later.)
- Create food-foraging opportunities. (Refer to chapter 6.)
- Let kitty explore the garage or attic if it's safe.
- Set a narrow board across two chairs to simulate walking across a fence.

Pretty simple, right? You don't need a harness, a stroller, or chicken wire to access the natural world and reap its benefits. "By creating an indoor environment that mimics or helps to duplicate the cat's natural state, we can satisfy both physical and emotional needs," pet behavior consultant Amy Shojai says. "That reduces stress, which, in turn, can reduce or eliminate stress-related behavior problems that loving cat owners unintentionally inflict on their pets."

Scent Enrichment

Our noses aren't as sensitive as cats', so the smells we encounter daily don't affect us as much unless they're very strong ones. We'll notice the odor of a litter box that hasn't been cleaned in days, for example, or we'll take note of the scent of freshly baked cookies wafting in from the kitchen. Smell is incredibly important to our feline friends, though, so we need to provide them with opportunities to sniff out new things.

One way to do this is to simply open a screened-in window and let the natural scents of earth and rain and even the neighbor's dog excite our cats' noses. "In the spring, when I open the windows after they've been closed for the winter, my cats are plastered up against the screen just because of all those outdoor smells," Adelman says. "It's smell o' vision."

However, letting your cat onto the porch, walking her on a harness, taking her for a ride in a stroller, or giving her access to a catio is another way to ensure that she can sniff to her heart's content.

There are plenty of indoor scent-enrichment opportunities as well. You're no doubt familiar with catnip, which about 70–80 percent of cats respond to. But silver vine is another olfactory stimulant that can also bring on a euphoric state, and it's even more potent because it contains two cat attractants. So sprinkling a bit of this on a favorite toy will no doubt entice even the sleepiest of cats to roll around and play.

And there's no shortage of items around the house, especially in the kitchen, that felines will want to investigate. Even if you discourage your cat from "helping out" when you're cooking, you've likely found it difficult to dissuade your cat from sniffing and sampling. Why? Because it smells so tempting! We may assume that kitty is after a snack, but often, they're just curious.

"A lot of times it's because food, especially, has very strong smells, and cats just want to investigate," Adelman observes. "So typically, when I'm preparing food or cooking, if anything that I'm preparing is safe for the cat, I just hold down a little bit so that they can smell it. Ninety percent of the time they smell it and walk away. Ten percent of the time they grab it and eat it, and that's why I only hold down things that are safe. But if I offer it to them, if I hold it down toward the floor, they don't need to jump up on the counter and walk across my cutting board."

That's why whenever Adelman is cooking, you're likely to see a cat nearby batting a sprig of rosemary (rosemary is safe for cats to eat). But foods aren't the only smelly items her cats have access to. Plenty of household items also exude scents that intrigue her felines, so she makes sure to give them time with those as well.

"Everything smells interesting to a cat," she says. "I throw my junk mail on the floor for fifteen minutes before I put it in the recycling

bin. They also love the laundry when it comes out of the dryer, so I have a towel that I put in the dryer with my other laundry. That's the cats' towel. So when I take the laundry out, I throw that on the floor. It's warm, and it smells cool, and they love it, so when I'm doing the laundry, they get the catch."

Of course, you certainly don't want the floor of your home covered in herbs, political mailers, and towels, but cats often need only a few minutes to check out something that's smelly, new, and exciting. That rosemary smells of nature, and the mail has been touched by different people and sat in the mailbox. Cats just want a little while to experience something new, but the novelty will wear off—"Usually they're done with the junk mail in five minutes," Adelman notes—and then you can toss it or put it away, knowing you've made your cat's day a little more interesting.

Change

If you stayed at home during the pandemic, you're well aware that it didn't take long for the days to bleed into one another. Soon, weekends felt just like weekdays, and even leaving the house to run an errand—to get groceries or run to the post office—was suddenly exciting. Finally, somewhere to go! Something new to see!

As we now know, our indoor cats essentially live as if there's a permanent pandemic. Very rarely does anything in their environment change. And when it does—when you bring the scents of the outdoors in on your shoes, when you open the door to a rarely used closet, when you get out the toolbox for a little home repair and there are nails to bat and screws to chase—your cat is right there to get in on the action.

"It's just like anything else [in life]," Robinson says. "Like if Netflix only offered two shows and you had to watch those over and over again, how excited would you be? That's why people have different games on their iPad. We just have to constantly think and change it up for our cats."

Cats grow and change over time, and their enrichment should, too.

So make your cat's life a little different every day. Let him explore a new cabinet. Rearrange the furniture. Toss a treat down the hall. Drape a sheet over a table to create a fort. Throw some junk mail on the floor. Open a different window. Place an ice cube in the bathtub for him to chase. Let him discover a wine cork or an empty toilet paper roll. It doesn't have to be anything grand, expensive, or time-consuming. Just get creative and you'll learn that the possibilities are endless.

Cats also require another type of change, though. They need their environment and their types of enrichment to adapt to their changing needs as they age. "Cats grow and change over time, so it's important to remember that," Purrcast cohost Sara Iyer says.

For example, the same type of toys may not appeal to both kittens and adult cats, just as a short scratching post is perfect for a kitten while an older cat requires a taller one, so he can get in a full stretch. The same goes for litter boxes. While a top-entry box or one with high sides works well for young felines, older cats are prone to arthritis and often need litter boxes with easier entry, such as lower sides or a ramp.

So consider your cat's age, life stage, or even changing interests. Remember that there was once a time when you were disappointed to receive socks as a gift or you dreaded the approach of naptime? But now? Some fluffy socks and a mandatory nap? Absolutely!

Cat TV

We enjoy settling in to watch some good television now and then, and our cats are the same way. But instead of bingeing *Schitt's Creek* or rewatching *Gilmore Girls* for the 10th time (hey, no judgment from us), our feline friends prefer reality TV. And we're not talking *The Bachelor* and *The Great British Bake Off*. We're talking birds and squirrels and maybe the occasional chipmunk.

Luckily, there's no cable subscription required to provide your cat with high-quality feline television. All you need is an accessible window. This could be a perch you attach to the window, or it could be as simple as sliding a couch, a desk, or another piece of furniture in front of it so kitty can see.

You can make it even more exciting and engaging by setting up a birdfeeder outside to attract lots of entertainment. Don't have a yard to do that? No problem. Get a feeder that attaches to the

window with suction cups to bring winged visitors up close and personal. Or simply put a bowl of birdseed on your balcony or fire escape. Once word gets out that you're providing snacks for the local wildlife, your window will get plenty of visitors, which means quality entertainment for your indoor cat.

YouTube also has a wealth of "cat-tastic" television options. Simply search for CAT TV, BIRDS FOR CATS TO WATCH, or anything along these lines, and you'll be rewarded with hours upon hours of video that kitty can tune into anytime. Play it on a computer, tablet, phone, or your television set, but keep an eye on your cat if they're watching on the big screen. We know from experience that when cats are stalking their prey, they may attempt to pounce—and you'll all appreciate keeping the TV in one piece.

Toys

Our taste in "toys" changes as we age. At one time we may have wanted dolls, trucks, and action figures, but as we grew up, we wanted different things, like clothes, iPhones, and concert tickets. Once again, cats aren't that different from us.

No, the senior Mr. Whiskers isn't longing for Taylor Swift tickets (although Swift would probably love to meet him). But just because Mr. Whiskers is all grown up doesn't mean that he doesn't still want and need to play.

Oftentimes, cat owners purchase a slew of toys when their cat is young or new to their home, but as the cat gets older, develops new interests, and begins to play differently, new toys are brought into the home far less often. Part of the problem is that there's a false perception that older cats don't play. But there's also an assumption that just because a cat has some toys, or entertains himself with objects he finds around the house, that he's set for life. This isn't the case, though.

Even as adults, we purchase "toys" for ourselves all the time—everything from movies and books to gaming systems and cars—and adult cats yearn for new items as well. So in addition to playing with your cat daily, a dedicated kitty caregiver should also bring a new plaything into their cats' lives frequently.

These new toys don't have to be expensive. In fact, they don't even have to be store-bought. Google DIY CAT TOYS, and you'll find a multitude of handmade options. If you'd rather purchase toys, though, we strongly suggest that you forgo a lot of the colorful items you'll find at big-box pet stores and instead do a little research and look into more innovative and unique cat toys.

The toys you'll frequently find in large retail stores are made to catch the attention of people. After all, we're the ones being marketed to. And while there are some undeniably hilarious and adorable cat toys available today, they tend to appeal to us, rather than to cats. Surely we're not the only ones who've purchased sparkling wand toys and avocado-shaped cat toys that our feline friends have zero interest in actually playing with.

So regularly shop with your cat in mind and keep your kitty dream home filled with novel items that invite kitty to stalk, swat, and pounce.

Do This, Not That

DO place cushions, toys, and catnip or silver vine atop bookshelves and other high-up areas to draw your cat to vertical space.

DON'T allow your cat access to potentially dangerous areas where he might get hurt.

DO purchase or make a new toy each month—not just during holidays or on your cat's birthday or "Gotcha Day."

DON'T leave interactive toys out—bring them out only when you're playing with your cat.

DO rotate toys.

DON'T continually put non-interactive toys away. If you want to keep things tidy, rotate toys or keep baskets of toys in various rooms.

DO move furniture beneath a window to create an instant perch to watch Cat TV.

DON'T assume that you have to purchase brand-new items to create a kitty playland.

Interaction

If your cat were to envision his dream home, you would be a central part of it. No, not just your ability to open cans of food and create an incredibly warm and comfortable lap, but *you*, his human companion.

Research shows that cats form attachments to their owners that are similar to those that dogs and even infants form with their caregivers. "The majority of cats are looking to their owners to be a source of safety and security," says Kristyn Vitale, whose study on the attachment between cats and humans was published in the journal *Current Biology* in 2019. "It's important for owners to think about that. When they're in a stressful situation, how they're behaving can actually have a direct impact on their cats' behavior."

While clean litter boxes, interactive toys, scratching posts, and everything else we've covered in this chapter are essential to a cat's well-being, you—the very person holding this book—are as well. You cared enough to pick up a book about indoor cats and read it, so the felines in your life are very lucky indeed.

So continue to give your cat more of what you're already giving her: love, snuggles, attention, playtime, cuddles.

"Make time to connect," Steven Ray Morris says. "Just time to hang out and be like, 'Who's the baby? You're the baby.' That kind of stuff. You just have to look your cat in the eye every once in a while and be like, 'Hey, man, I see you' and nom on those beans a little bit. There are times I realize I'm maybe not feeling as connected to [my cat] Penny Lane as I want to be, so I make time to catch up with her. We'll hang out in bed, and I'll just squish her a little bit, give her some smooches and just listen, and we'll tell each other about our days."

And don't forget to give your kitty plenty of slow blinks. Yes, your cat communicates her contentment when she blinks slowly, but you can do the same to your cat by smiling at her and saying,

"I love you, too." Sure, we already knew it and did it, too, but science confirmed it in 2020 through a study at the University of Sussex in the UK.

"As someone who has both studied animal behavior and is a cat owner, it's great to be able to show that cats and humans can communicate in this way," says psychologist Karen McComb, who supervised the University of Sussex research on felines' slow-blinking behavior. "It's something that many cat owners had already suspected, so it's exciting to have found evidence for it."

Myth: Cat Scratchers and Trees Are Ugly and Expensive

A common complaint from cat owners is that outfitting their home for kitty requires sacrificing the look and style of the home, but this doesn't have to be the case. Not all cat trees are carpeted monstrosities that come in varying shades of brown.

Today, there are a variety of sleek, chic, and downright stylish cat trees on the market that can do more than simply blend into your home décor—they can actually enhance it.

And if you can't find one that fits the bill, make your own. That's what Martin Henrion did when he wanted a piece of kitty furniture that both he and his cats would love. What inspired him?

"It was probably equal parts design aesthetics and for the cats," he recalls. "The cats really love looking out this window at the neighboring Poinciana tree, which attracts a lot of birds, but I wanted to have something more natural-looking in the house than a carpeted cat tree."

Henrion's DIY cat tree is constructed from found native wood and held together with nothing but wood glue and dowels as connectors. It features platforms, scratching areas, and even a little hammock. He estimates that it cost him less than $200 and took him about 40 hours of build time because he was "figuring some things out along the way.

"I didn't have any plans or guides to work from, but I had a vision in mind to begin with: three branches of different heights to give it a forest-like appearance," he says.

The finished cat tree is truly a work of art. Best of all? His two cats, Gandalf the White and Radagast the Brown, are *obsessed* with it.

CHAPTER 14

The Feline Future

Your POV: I want to do better for my cat.	Kitty POV: Thank you.

As pet parents, we're not perfect. We make mistakes. Perhaps now you've realized that enclosing your cat in four walls for his or her entire life was a mistake on your part. The very reason we all welcomed felines into our lives and shut the door is because we wanted them to be safe and happy, right?

But that isn't the full picture. Keeping our cats indoors wasn't only to protect them or even to protect the local wildlife. We also did it for ourselves. We have to at least acknowledge that our reasoning also serves our own best interests. The bonds we develop with our cats are stronger when we live together, so the decision to keep our felines close is also a selfish one.

The question we want each kitty caregiver to consider is this: Are we putting our own interests above those of the cats we love? It's a complicated question with an even more complicated answer.

The truth is that the history of domestic cats in the United States is one of extremes. Felines went from free-roaming outdoor animals to kept indoor family members that we, both intentionally

and inadvertently, stripped of their choices when we shut them inside. Unable to explore, hunt, walk on grass, feel the sun on their fur—and often unable to even engage in natural behaviors like scratching—we've essentially denied cats the chance to truly be cats.

And even the life of *felis interius* is one of extremes. As an indoor-only kitty, too often we see this feline living one of two lives: that of an overly babied social media star, dressed in costumes like a prop, or that of the "low-maintenance" pet, overlooked and left alone at home for days on end with just a lone litter box and a bowl full of dry kibble. Again, this is not the natural cat.

But we can do better. Sure, we'll continue to make mistakes along the way. But changing our perspective about what cats need and deserve will help us bridge this gap between what cats *are* and what we've tried to make them become.

After spending the majority of 2020 trapped within our own four walls, we're in a unique position to understand the plight of the indoor cat. And if we take that understanding a step further and truly empathize with our beloved pets, we can take action and transform our cats' lives. We can allow our feline friends to tap into their true nature.

Not only will this improve the lives of our beloved pets, but it'll also help save the lives of community cats.

"I think American animal advocates would probably do well to broaden their perspectives on what a good life for a cat can be," Shaw says. "The notion that cats can only be successful when they're inside is not just damaging to individual cats who then are truly captive in our homes, but it's also damaging to the way that we manage animal populations in our municipalities. It causes cats to die by the hundreds of thousands simply because either they're not suitable for indoor homes or because there are numbers of cats seeking homes that exceed the volume of homes that are available. I think it's really crucial that we broaden our perspective on what a suitable home or what a good life for a cat can be."

For free-roaming and community cats, a good life could be defined simply as a *right* to life. While there are harsh critics who don't believe these animals should live outdoors, the fact is that the nation's sentiments are on the side of cats. In fact, 84 percent of Americans prefer that their tax dollars be used toward trap-neuter-return (TNR) programs—which involve trapping, spaying and/or neutering, and then returning these felines back into their environment to reduce their numbers—rather than capturing outdoor cats and euthanizing them.

And for the felines we share our homes and our lives with, a good life is simply one that more closely resembles the life of a natural cat. So we must embrace who our cats are. This means permitting them to engage in instinctive behaviors, like scratching, providing them with endless enrichment opportunities, and opening up their worlds to the very environment they came from.

We understand that letting your cat outside, even under your watchful eye or on a leash, is a decision that's fraught with worry and, unfortunately, even shame. We've been inundated with messaging that says cats should be indoors at all times, that it's what's best for them, that to do otherwise is to put your cat's life at risk and to open yourself up to judgment from neighbors, veterinary professionals, and perhaps even the very shelter or rescue that you adopted your cat from.

But again, we're not suggesting that you throw open the door and let your cat wander freely. We're simply asking that you recognize who and what your cat is and allow him to be that and express that.

What we hope this book helps accomplish is the establishment of a happy medium for our feline friends. It's not all or nothing, inside or outside. We believe there's a middle ground and that the person best equipped to make decisions about each individual feline is the caregiver who knows them and loves them.

Recognize who and what your cat is and allow him to be that and express that.

This may mean that your cat gets to wander the backyard while you sip your morning coffee. It could mean constructing a catio that your kitties can lounge in each afternoon. Or it could mean simply opening a screened-in window to let in birdsong, direct sunlight, and all the fascinating scents of the outdoor world. In other words, it's up to you. Your cat's health and happiness are your responsibility, and you've known that all along.

After all, there are a few questions that cat owners ask us again and again, and we have no doubt you've pondered them yourself:

- Is my cat happy?
- Does my cat love me?
- Does my cat know that I love her?

By now, we're sure you can answer the first one. There are numerous ways to assess your cat's happiness.

- Is your cat in good physical health?
- Does she have a healthy appetite?
- Does she use the litter box?
- Does she play?
- Is she interested in her environment?
- Does she purr?
- What's her body language like? Does she seem pleased to see you?
- Does she rub on you? Knead near or on you? Groom you?
- How much of the day does she spend sleeping?

The question we want you to ask, though, is this: Could your cat be happier? The answer is very likely yes. And if you've read this far, you no doubt want that for your kitty.

Clearly, your kitty-loving heart is in the right place, and you now have the knowledge and tools to give your cat an even better life. Taking what you've learned from this book and putting these ideas into action will allow you to answer that third question: Does my cat know I love her?

Because when you're willing to put your cat's best interests above your own, your feline friend will reap the benefits and know without a doubt that you love her (or him).

What Does the Feline Future Look Like?

From a cultural perspective, the outlook for felines is certainly positive. With millions of cat videos on the internet and an estimated 6.5 billion cat photos already online, felines truly rule the internet. Cats haven't only taken over YouTube and Instagram, though; they've also conquered our homes. In fact, there are nearly 100 million pet cats in the United States, making them the most "pawpular" pet in the nation.

"I think the biggest benefit of cat culture becoming more mainstream is going to be for cats themselves," says Steven Ray Morris, pointing toward the popularity of cats on social media, the increasing number of cat-related conventions happening across the United States, and the success of adopt-don't-shop campaigns. "We're going to see more adoptions and fewer cats on the street. And then cats who are on the street are going to be more accepted and hopefully safer because of TNR and how our understanding of cats has improved. So I think, overall, the lives of cats are just going to get better."

As for the future of *felis interius*, though, there's a lot to consider. And, honestly, there's a lot we just don't know yet.

What we do know is that we are changing cats. We've been doing it for some time. After all, cat domestication occurred as a result of agricultural development and formed a mutually beneficial relationship with humans. "Nothing about the process was intentional," writes Rebecca J. Rosen in an *Atlantic* article titled "How Humans Created Cats." "No human set out to try to domesticate a cat or a dog and make it into a pet, but a chain reaction was set off by a human practice, and one thing led to another, and our pets today are the result."

When we consider how our relationship with cats and their domestication came to be, in a way, it evolved somewhat naturally. We didn't intentionally select for desired traits and breed ourselves the ideal feline companion. If we had, surely we would've bred out the domestic cat's propensity for midnight zoomies and 3 a.m. feedings.

But what we are doing is creating *felius interius*. Perhaps unwittingly, we've selected for the kind of felines we want in our homes. "We're going to somehow select for cats that have less desire to roam and are a little bit less active and that are more adaptable to being indoors," Adelman says.

Right now, the felines who adjust to life indoors, who become little more than adorable lap warmers and ornaments to adorn our homes, are the ones who will remain. The ones that deny their nature and the ones that clearly struggle to adapt to this manufactured lifestyle—those that act out, become aggressive, anxiously overgroom, or eliminate outside the litter box—are much more likely to be abandoned or relinquished. They're much more likely

to never find another home and to be euthanized, along with millions of other healthy cats in US shelters.

Cats that are sociable and easily or instantly take to indoor life might sound appealing. You could even make the argument that it would be easier for shelters to adopt out such animals. But we can't help but raise this question: Is the indoor cat—is *felis interius*—still truly a cat?

As you consider this matter, we have a few other questions for you to ponder:

What do we want from our cats? Do we want the natural cat, or do we want a pet that more closely resembles an ornament in our homes?

Is an indoor-only lifestyle doing our cats more harm than good?

As *felis interius* adapts to the environment we've forced upon the species and becomes less natural, will our attachment to them begin to wane? Will we view them like a fish in a tank, something beautiful we like to observe but with little emotional attachment? Or will this proximity lead to an even stronger human–animal bond?

And, finally, what will domestic cats look like a generation from now? In 50 years? In 100?

We truly believe that the answer to this last question is up to people like you, the ones who love their own felines and others enough to read an entire book on the subject. So we challenge you to think and to act. And we implore you to please open up your cat's world, even if you just open a window.

ACKNOWLEDGMENTS

I have so many people (and cats) to thank, but I've already written thousands of words so I'll try to keep this brief.

First, Lynn, thank you for trusting me with this book, and thank you for your friendship, encouragement, and continuous inspiration. You've taught me so much and I aspire to be as compassionate and generous as you are.

To Corey Wright, Jamie Brooks, Kristen Bobst, Andrea Cunningham, Birdy Jones, Debbie Burns, Salima Alikhan, Natalia Meja-Saldarriaga, and Shannon Moss, thanks for cheering me on, keeping me sane, and helping me not feel so alone, as I wrote this entire manuscript during a seemingly endless quarantine. Only one of you shares a last name with me, but you're all family.

Myrsini Stephanides, thank you so much for believing in this book when it was just a rambling email. Also, thank you, little Carson, for sharing your brilliant mother with Lynn and me so we could bring this to life.

Jordana Hawkins and Jennifer Kasius, your vision, guidance, and hard work made *Indoor Cat* a reality. Your editorial "purrowess" is all over this book and it's better because of it, so thanks to you and to everyone at Running Press who lent a paw.

Thanks to Java Cats Café for keeping me caffeinated as I wrote the proposal for this book and drafted the first chapters. And Hadyn Hilton, thanks for creating a space so full of compassion, creativity, generosity, and, of course, coffee.

Also, thanks and purrs to those who shared their knowledge, insights, and felines with us to create *Indoor Cat*: Karen Nguyen, Martin Henrion, Ashley McFarland, Lyndsey Lewis, Rose Rosenhauer, Christopher Bobst, Kathy Copeland, Niki Malek, Hannah Shaw, Steven Ray Morris, Sara Iyer, Dr. Jennifer Conrad, Dr. Patricia Lane,

Acknowledgments

Dr. Lisa Radosta, Dr. Robin Downing, Dr. Joe Bartges, Dr. Rolan Tripp, Dr. Andrea Tasi, Dr. Tony Buffington, Dr. Alice Villabobos, Steve Dale, Amy Shojai, Ingrid King, Becky Robinson, Pam Johnson-Bennett, Jodi Ziskin, Beth Adelman, Daniel Quagliozzi, Dana Widmer, Lori Shepler, Deb Barnes, Sandra Samman, Jeremy Ernst-Verhime, Richard Jung, Kate Benjamin, Dr. Laura Cochran, and Sandy Robbins.

To everyone who follows *Adventure Cats* and has supported us over the years, thank you as well. You and your fearless felines inspire me every day.

Thank you, dear reader, for picking this book up because you want to give your own indoor cat the best "pawsible" nine lives.

And, finally, many thanks to the feline loves of my life: Fiver, Sirius, and Screaming Travis. You enrich my life every day, and you—and all indoor cats—deserve the same.

—Laura

This book was written in honor of one of the greatest loves of my life, Rudolph, an amazing pink-nosed kitty who rocked my world. He was my first feline love, soul mate, and guide into the world of cats. Like Cupid's arrow, Rudolph took aim at my heart and filled it with unconditional love and devotion. He instilled in me a passion for all things cat-related and became my mentor, companion, confidant, educator, and role model. He taught me how to speak cat fluently. Like a bolt of lightning, Rudolph illuminated and altered the course of my life in ways I never could have imagined. I owe my career to this amazing gray and white ball of fluff who graciously entered my life and left an indelible mark on it. For that, I am eternally grateful.

Thank you, Laura Moss, for saying yes to collaborating with me because without you this book would not have come to fruition. I could not think of anyone else I would rather have partnered with. Your friendship, insights, knowledge, and experience made our journey writing this book together fun, enjoyable, interesting, and easy. I am in awe of your talents and am grateful that you shared them with me. Thank you for helping me find my voice and for turning my words into magic. Thank you for your support, encouragement, optimism, hard work, and enthusiasm in wanting to help cat owners become better pet parents. Working with you has been a privilege and an honor, and you made this a wonderful experience that I will never forget.

The inspiration to explore the specific needs of indoor cats came from Dezi and Roo, my current beloved kitties. Like a tsunami, these two magnificent creatures overtook my life and turned it upside down and inside out. They are my guides and muses, and it is because of them that I've dedicated myself to keeping indoor cats happy and healthy.

The insights I gained into the feline perspective, which I shared throughout this book, were compiled from my life's experience of working with and caring for thousands of felines as a veterinarian. It is because of them, and the people who love them, that I was inspired to write this book. I owe a debt of gratitude to each and every cat (and their humans) who crossed my path, touched my heart, and taught me about the power, strength, and beauty of the human–animal bond. This book is for them.

Many, many thanks to all my esteemed friends and colleagues who contributed their time, knowledge, and expertise to this book. Thank you, Dr. Patricia Lane, Dr. Lisa Radosta, Dr. Jennifer Conrad, Dr. Robin Downing, Dr. Joe Bartges, Dr. Rolan Tripp, Dr. Andrea Tasi, Dr. Tony Buffington, Dr. Alice Villabobos, Dr. Laura Cochran, Steve Dale, Amy Shojai, Ingrid King, Becky Robinson, Pam Johnson-Bennett, Jodi Ziskin, Beth Adelman, Richard Jung, Daniel Quagliozzi, Dana Widmer, Lori Shepler, Niki Malek, Deb Barnes, Sandra Samman, Jeremy Ernst-Verhime, Karen Nguyen, Hannah Shaw, Steven Ray Morris, Sara Iyer, Kate Benjamin, and Sandy Robbins. I am so proud to know each one of you and humbled by your kindness, generosity, support, and willingness to help. You are all pawsome!

To Myrsini Stephanides, agent extraordinaire, thank you for believing in our vision right from the start and for holding our hands throughout this journey. Your guidance, friendship, and encouragement were all instrumental in helping bring this book to life. Thank you so much.

Many thanks to the entire team at Running Press, led by our acclaimed editors, Jordana Hawkins and Jennifer Kasius, who made this book a reality.

A million, trillion, bazillion thanks to my husband, Brooks, for giving me the time, space, and encouragement needed to pursue this dream, and to my son, Alexander, for being my biggest fan and cheering me on along the way. Your love and unwavering support lifted me to heights I did not know existed. To say that I feel like the luckiest and richest girl in the world would be an understatement. Thank you from the bottom of my heart.

—Lynn

BIBLIOGRAPHY

Ahola, Milla K., Katariina Vapalahti, and Hannes Lohi. "Early Weaning Increases Aggression and Stereotypic Behaviour in Cats." *Scientific Reports*, September 4, 2017. https://www.nature.com/articles/s41598-017-11173-5.

Dell'Amore, Christine. "What Do Cats Think about Us? You May Be Surprised." *National Geographic*, February 10, 2021. https://www.nationalgeographic.com/adventure/article/140127-cats-pets-animals-nation-dogs-people-science.

Gorman, James. "Why Scientists Love to Study Dogs (and Often Ignore Cats)." *New York Times*, February 26, 2018. https://www.nytimes.com/2018/02/26/science/dog-science-cats.html.

Huck, Maren, and Samantha Watson. "The Use of Animal-Borne Cameras to Video-Track the Behavior of Domestic Cats." *Applied Animal Behaviour Science*, April 4, 2019. https://derby.openrepository.com/bitstream/handle/10545/623824/10.1016%40j.applanim.2019.04.016.pdf.

Lynn, William S., Arian Wallach, and Francisco J. Santiago-Ávila. "Don't Blame Cats for Killing Wildlife—Shaky Logic Is Creating a Moral Panic." *EcoWatch*, August 3, 2020. https://www.ecowatch.com/cats-killing-wildlife-2646869888.html?rebelltitem=1#rebelltitem1.

McGowan, Ragen T. S., Jacklyn J. Ellis, Miles K. Bensky, and François Martin. "The Ins and Outs of the Litter Box: A Detailed Ethogram of Cat Elimination Behavior in Two Contrasting Environments." *Applied Animal Behaviour Science* 194 (2017): 67–78. https://doi.org/10.1016/j.applanim.2017.05.009.

Montague, M. J., G. Li, B. Gandolfi, R. Khan, B. L. Aken, S. M. Searle, P. Minx, L. W. Hillier, D. C. Koboldt, B. W. Davis, C. A.

Driscoll, C. S. Barr, K. Blackistone, J. Quilez, B. Lorente-Galdos, T. Marques-Bonet, C. Alkan, G. W. Thomas, M. W. Hahn, M. Menotti-Raymond, S. J. O'Brien, R. K. Wilson, L. A. Lyons, W. J. Murphy, and W. C. Warren, "Comparative Analysis of the Domestic Cat Genome Reveals Genetic Signatures Underlying Feline Biology and Domestication." *Proceedings of the National Academy of Sciences of the United States of America*. U.S. National Library of Medicine, 2014. https://pubmed.ncbi.nlm.nih.gov/25385592/.

O'Neill, D. G., D. B. Church, P. D. McGreevy, P. C. Thomson, and D. C. Brodbelt. "Longevity and Mortality of Cats Attending Primary Care Veterinary Practices in England." *Journal of Feline Medicine and Surgery*. U.S. National Library of Medicine. https://pubmed.ncbi.nlm.nih.gov/24925771/.

Picheta, Rob. "Women Less Likely to Date Men with Cats, Study Finds." Cable News Network, June 22, 2020. https://www.cnn.com/2020/06/22/world/cat-men-dating-study-scli-intl-scn-wellness/index.html.

Rosen, Rebecca J. "How Humans Created Cats." *Atlantic*, March 30, 2018. https://www.theatlantic.com/technology/archive/2013/12/how-humans-created-cats/282391/.

Slivka, Kelly. "Kitty Cam Shows Not All Cats Are Killers." *New York Times*, August 8, 2012. https://green.blogs.nytimes.com/2012/08/08/kitty-cam-shows-not-all-cats-are-killers/.

Smith, Casey. "Cats Domesticated Themselves, Ancient DNA Shows." *National Geographic*, February 10, 2021. https://www.nationalgeographic.com/science/article/domesticated-cats-dna-genetics-pets-science.

Titeux, E., C. Gilbert, A. Briand, and N. Cochet-Faivre. "From Feline Idiopathic Ulcerative Dermatitis to Feline Behavioral Ulcerative Dermatitis: Grooming Repetitive Behaviors

Indicators of Poor Welfare in Cats." *Frontiers in Veterinary Science*. U.S. National Library of Medicine. https://pubmed.ncbi.nlm.nih.gov/29713639/.

Wolf, Peter. "What's Several Billion Birds, Among Friends?" *Vox Felina*, September 26, 2016. http://www.voxfelina.com/2016/09/whats-several-billion-birds-among-friends/.

PHOTO CREDITS

INDEX

Index

Index